Noël Graveline
Photographs by Francis Debai
Design Mireille Debaisieux

The Romanesque Treasures of the Auvergne

Editions DEBAISIEUX

CONTENTS

The basilica of Brioude (Haute-Loire), at night.

"Nous appelons époque romane le temps où la vie chrétienne s'ordonne en une civilisation et où l'union de l'architecture avec la sculpture et les arts qui vont devenir mineurs prend l'éclat des passages privilégiés de l'homme."

André Malraux,
Le Musée imaginaire
(t. 3 Le Monde chrétien)

The Madonna of Orcival (Puy-de-Dôme).

> *"Ils ne demandaient pas à un Crucifix d'être plus beau qu'un autre, mais d'être davantage le Christ, et la beauté suivait."*
>
> *André Malraux*

The Auzon Crucifix (Haute-Loire).

Saint John, in the Gannat Gospel-book (Puy-de-Dôme).

NPRIN
RATVER
ERAT APUD DM
BUM HOC ERAT

It is through its Romanesque art that the Auvergne has best reflected the nature of its people. This is true for the most humble chapel in the Cantal and the magnificent basilicas of the Limagne. These buildings, whose simple beauty appears to emerge from the soil to serve the highest spirituality, reflect a people which has long held the memory of its Arverne origins, whilst enriching its Roman heritage, before embracing artistic movements from the rest of Christendom. The Auvergnat likes to build solid buildings with no superfluity, and it was for this reason that, as from the beginning of the 11th century, the builders of churches in the province, came up with ingenious solutions which caught on. The forerunners then combined geometry with harmony, the main success of which are the chevets that are among the pinnacles of western architecture. This primordial art is often combined with typically Auvergnat sculpture and no less original statuary, with its black Madonnas and its Crucifixes.

The humble chapel of Chastel-sur-Murat (Cantal).

For many, the most attractive Romanesque churches in the Auvergne are discrete, mountain shrines. Nevertheless, it is the architecture of the important churches of the Limagne which best reflects the specific character of the art that the builders of this region developed from the 10th century onwards. We note first that the plan of these churches is remarkably sophisticated, following a development which drew on Antiquity and the Carolingian tradition. The classic form of a Latin cross pointing east is completed by a narthex and absidioles positioned on each arm of the transept and, in particular, an ambulatory, generally with radial chapels, the most important innovation of the Auvergnat master builders to allow pilgrims to file past religious relics. Such refinement gives buildings of relatively modest dimensions a monumental aspect.

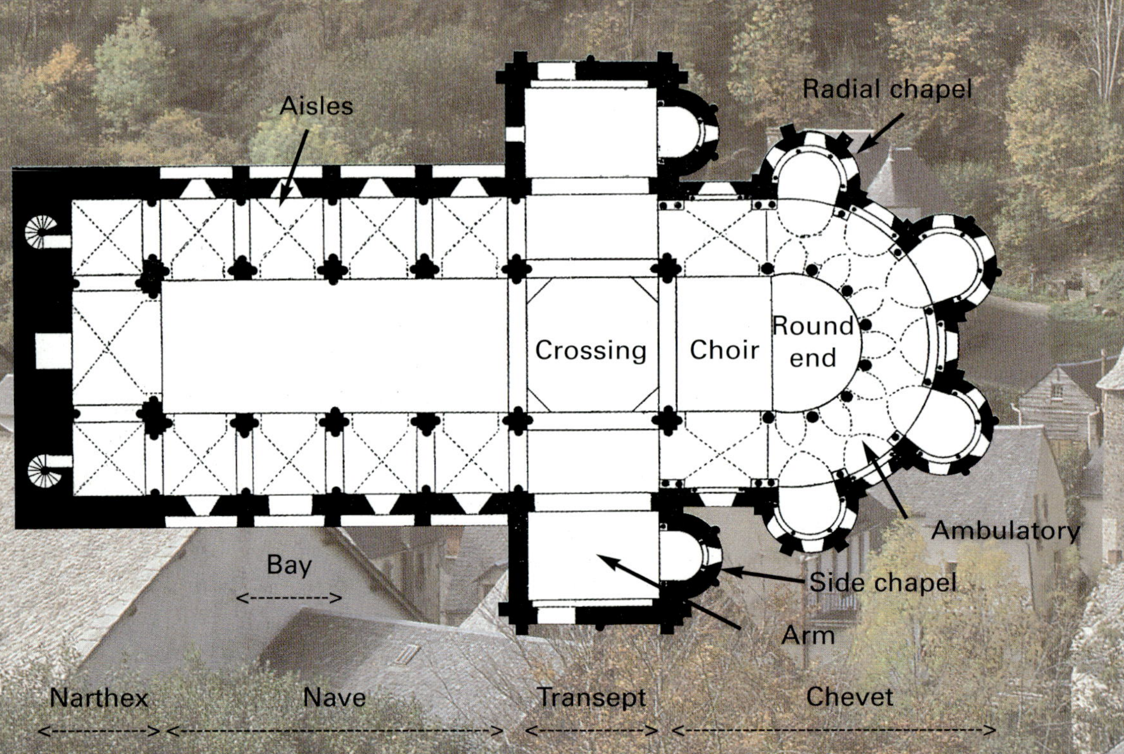

Plan sketched by the Reverend Bernard Craplet, drawn by Dom Noël Deney. L'Auvergne romane. Zodiaque

Architectural features

Orcival

"Orcival : blotti dans la vallée comme au creux d'une paume, à la convergence des plis."

Jean Anglade,
Mémoires d'Auvergne. De Borée

Saint-Nectaire (Puy-de-Dôme), the perfect profile of Romanesque churches in the Auvergne.

Spire of bell tower
Cupola
Diaphragm arch
Tower
Gallery
Choir
Crossing
Bay
Gallery
Narthex

Section sketched by the Reverend Bernard Craplet, drawn by Dom Noël Deney. L'Auvergne romane. *Zodiaque*

Primitive churches were covered with roofs, which caused problems when it came to vaulting. Once again, the local builders innovated to reconcile the need for strength and light. The aisles were built with galleries topped by quadrant vaults that buttress the thrust of the main arch. Light enters through the windows of the lower level, which highlights the pillars and through those of the galleries, thanks to bays which provide light of surprising softness. The same principle applied to the transept crossing, which is topped by a cupola and bell tower, produced another distinctive feature, the "barlong" block. This terms refers to the raised part of the rectangular plane that provides lateral support for the pressure from the top sections, the many windows of which contribute to illuminating the nave. The light from the sky is increased inside by the presence of raised diaphragm arches which support the dome.

Below - *Nave of the church of Issoire (Puy-de-Dôme*
Opposite - *Diaphragm arches of the transept crossing of the church at Ennezat (Puy-de-Dôme).*

The Modesty of Mérimée

As an inspector of historical monuments, Prosper Mérimée travelled throughout France to draw up an inventory of the rich heritage of the country. When he came to the description of the modillions of the collegiate church at Ennezat in his Notes de Voyage, he refused to use anything other than Latin so much did he consider the sculptures of these decorations to be improper...

Above left - *The use of polychrome materials at Brioude (Haute-Loire).*
Right - *The sophisticated harmony of the chevet at Saint-Nectaire (Puy-de-Dôme).*

A billet course at Glaine-Montaigut (Puy-de-Dôme).

Finally, we come to the chevet, the greatest achievement of the local builders. All agree in praising the beauty and balance of the subtle layout of the volumes of this part of the building. As the eye travels over this remarkable architectural pyramid, it is attracted to the radiating chapels, the ambulatory and the apse, before rising to the transept, the "barlong" and the bell tower. Furthermore, chevets in the Auvergne use a wide range of decorative effects, chequerboards, rows of billets, modillions, flat buttresses and engaged columns.

Below left - *The pentagonal chevet at Roffiac (Cantal).*
Right - *Capitals and modillions at Bourg-Lastic (Puy-de-Dôme).*

Above - *Stone mosaics at Chauriat (Puy-de-Dôme).*
Right - *The typically Auvergnat "barlong" which caps the crossing of the transept and supports the bell-tower of the church of Saint-Austremoine at Issoire (Puy-de-Dôme).*

Below - *The apse covered with roofing stones of the mountain church at Orcival (Puy-de-Dôme).*
Opposite
Left - *Interlaced motifs on the apse at Ydes (Cantal).*
Right - *Naive modillions of the church at Dienne (Cantal).*

A Romanesque School in the Auvergne

The source of Romanesque art in the Auvergne is the cathedral that Bishop Etienne II gave to Clermont in 946, traces of which can still be seen in the crypt of the present Gothic shrine. This 10th century church was the first to have a chevet with an ambulatory and radiating chapels; a plan that was to have the success we are all familiar with. In about 1020, the primitive cathedral was replaced by a new Romanesque building, which was itself demolished in the 13th century to make way for the Gothic cathedral. It should be noted that until it was restored by Viollet-the-Duc, the Cathedral of Clermont retained its narthex and the sober west front of this prototype of the Auvergne Romanesque school.

On Mont Cornadore, the church of Saint-Nectaire (Puy-de-Dôme).

The Major Churches

The transept of Notre-Dame-du-Port. Opposite - *The door with its polychrome tympanum.*

Below, top - *Ilumination from the Clermont Bible (circa 1200).* Bottom - *Urbain II's call to the crusade in a 19th century image (BMIU Clermont-Ferrand).*

Notre-Dame-du-Port, a perfect unity of style

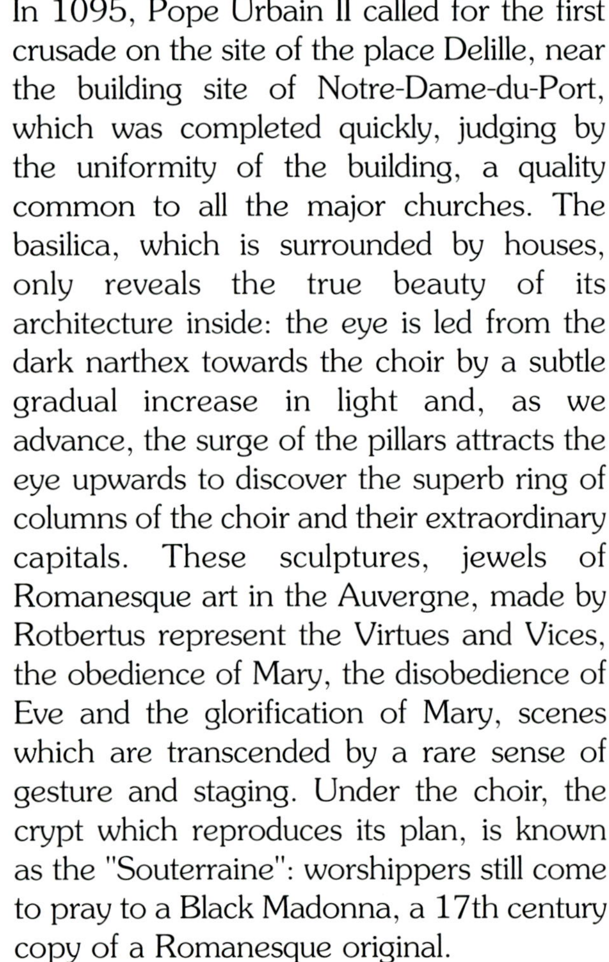

In 1095, Pope Urbain II called for the first crusade on the site of the place Delille, near the building site of Notre-Dame-du-Port, which was completed quickly, judging by the uniformity of the building, a quality common to all the major churches. The basilica, which is surrounded by houses, only reveals the true beauty of its architecture inside: the eye is led from the dark narthex towards the choir by a subtle gradual increase in light and, as we advance, the surge of the pillars attracts the eye upwards to discover the superb ring of columns of the choir and their extraordinary capitals. These sculptures, jewels of Romanesque art in the Auvergne, made by Rotbertus represent the Virtues and Vices, the obedience of Mary, the disobedience of Eve and the glorification of Mary, scenes which are transcended by a rare sense of gesture and staging. Under the choir, the crypt which reproduces its plan, is known as the "Souterraine": worshippers still come to pray to a Black Madonna, a 17th century copy of a Romanesque original.

The basilica of Notre-Dame-du-Port.

The round end of the choir of Notre-Dame-du-Port.

The Temptation of Eve, one of the best known capitals of the choir.

The Triumph of Benevolence and Charity, virtues in armour.

The crossing of the transept and its cupola.

Left - *Joseph being awakened from his dream by an angel.*
Centre - *The Black Madonna based on a 13th century icon.*
Right - *The foundation of the basilica with Stephanus the donator.*

The Romanesque frescos of the ambulatory of the crypt.

Below - *The 12th century Notre-Dame de la Bonne-Mort, which was painted black in the 19th century.*
Inset - *The Our Lady of Alleaume, the model for Auvergnat Madonnas, in a 12th century manuscript (BMIU Clermont-Ferrand).*

NOTRE-DAME DE-LA-BONNE-MORT

In 1974, a Romanesque Black Madonna was discovered in Clermont Cathedral, in the former bishops' mortuary chapel. This walnut statue, which was named Notre-Dame-de-la-Bonne-Mort, is now displayed in the side chapel. Judging by the gilding of her vestment, she is a reference to the Holy Virgin Mary. This Virgin, which disappeared during the Revolution, was ordered by Bishop Etienne II from the goldsmith Alleaume in 946. An effigy which was the oldest statue of the Blessed Virgin Mary known in Christendom.

Notre-Dame-de-la-Bonne-Mort belongs to the family of Auvergnat Black Madonnas, but her colour only dates back to the 19th century, which does nothing to diminish the evocative power of the Virgin and Child, which reflects both a remote immobility and profound humanity.

The Romanesque Treasures of the Cathedral of Clermont

Whether their pre-1000 AD model be the "first" black Madonna of The Puy or the enigmatic Madonna of Alleaume from the primitive cathedral of Clermont, Romanesque reliquary Madonnas are more common in the Auvergne than in any other province. These Madonnas with Child are always in Glory, that is they are on the "throne of wisdom" in a posture of eastern origin. Similarly, their expressions are always fascinating, with a mixture of hieratic style and gentleness which does not exclude a wide range of sources of inspiration. Madonnas may be represented as a transfigured peasant woman, with a mask from the dawn of time or as a simple girl touched by grace, a noble queen or a radiant goddess. All the Romanesque Madonnas in the Auvergne came from only two or three artists' workshops.

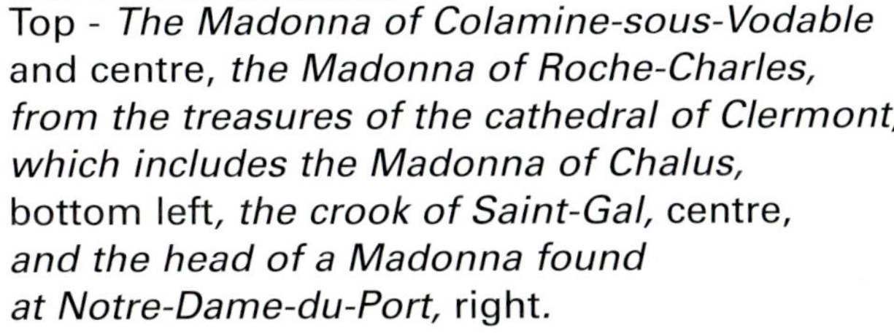

Top - *The Madonna of Colamine-sous-Vodable* and centre, *the Madonna of Roche-Charles, from the treasures of the cathedral of Clermont, which includes the Madonna of Chalus,* bottom left, *the crook of Saint-Gal,* centre, *and the head of a Madonna found at Notre-Dame-du-Port,* right.

An illuminated letter from the Clermont Bible, a Romanesque manuscript (Municipal and Inter-University Library of Clermont-Ferrand).

The Romanesque stained glass windows of the cathedral

The stained glass windows which light the chapel of Saint-Anne, the former bishops' mortuary, in the morning, include one of the finest groups of 12th century stained glass conserved in France. These stained glass windows, which were taken from the Romanesque Cathedral, were made between 1160 and 1200 and may have been donated by Saint Louis (Louis IX) for the wedding of his son. It was under the vaults of Clermont Cathedral that the future Philippe III "The Bold" married Isabella of Arragon, in 1262. Seen from bottom to top and from left to right, they trace the Childhood of Christ with, in particular, the Annunciation, the Birth of Christ, the Adoration of the Magi and the flight to Egypt. Half way up, two panels stand out from the series and show, on the right, Christ in majesty in a mandorla and, on the left, the Pentecost, with scarlet flames licking down on to the heads of the Apostles. The ten top panels should be excluded from this series, they are 13th century.

(*all the panels in the photograph are 12th century.)

The tympanum with the Virgin, Saint Pierre and his keys, and Saint Austremoine who is commending the kneeling abbot of Mozac.

The Saintes-Femmes, with disproportionately large heads, in accordance with Auvergnat tradition.

Mozac, the abbey church of Saint Calmin

Founded in about 680 by Calmin the Count of Auvergne, Mozac abbey received the relics of Saint Austremoine and became one of the main institutions in the province. The large Romanesque church around which the abbey was organised, was unfortunately destroyed by several earthquakes during the 15th century and the present building is a poor reflection of its former splendour. Nevertheless, the church at Mozac kept the reliquary of Saint Calmin, the most imposing example of 12th century Limousin gold and silver work left to us, together with superb capitals dating back to the golden age of Romanesque sculpture. Two of them represent the Resurrection and a group of Atlantes, whilst that of the Apocalypse, discovered recently, shows four Angels closing their mouths representing the Winds.

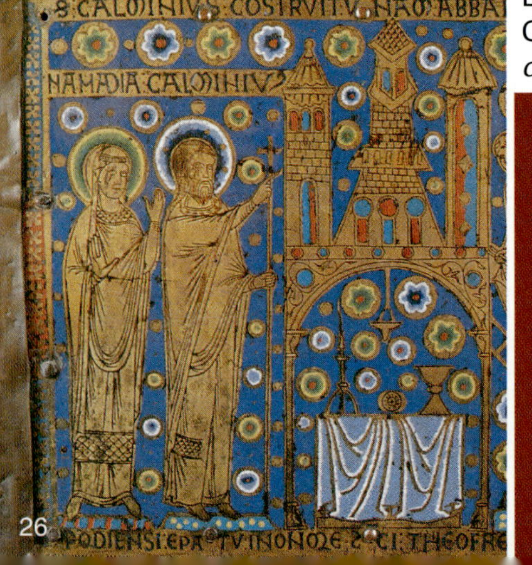

Below - *The reliquary of Saint Calmin in enamelled copper.*
Opposite - *A detail showing Saint Calmin and his wife during the construction of the monastery.*

The front of the church of Ennezat.

The "Cathedral of the marshes"

Unfortunately, at the east end of the church of Ennezat, a Gothic apse in Volvic stone replaced its Romanesque predecessor. Nevertheless, the ambition of the 13th century builders led to the interruption of work, thus saving the original nave and narthex, built in arkose, which are among the oldest examples of Romanesque art in the Limagne. The "Cathedral of the marshes" as it was christened as a reminder of the nature of the area during its construction, was one of the first to make use of the shoulder of the half barrel arches of the galleries, in about 1080, to support the thrust from the vaulting of the nave.

The money lender's torment

One of the best known capitals in the Auvergne, on the last pillar of the nave of the church of Ennezat, represents the torment of the money lender. Here, this theme, which is a familiar one in the province, is treated in the original prosaic style and was probably used as the model for all other regional representations of the evil rich.

The reverend Bernard Craplet, a specialist in Romanesque art in the Auvergne, analysed the capital as follows: "We see the money lender in Hell, naked as the damned. Two winged demons, with their hair on end, wearing animal-skin loin-cloths, are holding him by the hands and feet. Around his neck the leather purse in which he kept his gold and between his legs, on the ground, a jar in which he hid his treasure: MUNERA DIVE... The last few letters are illegible. A long banner is being waved in front of the characters by a small demon (on the left), whilst another (on the right), sitting on a stool, has just written the avenging text. Above him, attached to a strap, the horn which holds his ink. We read: CANDO USURAM ACCEPISTI OPERA MEA FECISTI. As a money lender, you worked for me."

Above - *The "Money lender's" capital.*
Below - *The galleried nave and, in the background, the narthex.*

The Free Mason's church

Another Romanesque shrine is located close to the famous church of Saint Julien at Chauriat, the former parish church of Saint Mary. This 11th and 12th century building was abandoned during the Revolution, and was sold to Claude Antoine Rudel du Miral, one of the members of the National Convention who voted to put Louis XVI to death. Whilst converting the church into a warehouse, the new owner, who was a Free Mason, engraved the masonic symbols of the ten pointed equilateral triangle and the five pointed star, in a niche in the bell tower and they can still be seen today.

Top - *The mosaics of the church at Chauriat.*
Bottom - *The crossing of the church Saint-Martin at Cournon.*
Inset - *At Chauriat, the capital of Christ washing the feet of Saint Pierre.*

Built of arkose, tuff and lava

The church of Saint-Julien de Chauriat, which was severely damaged by earthquakes during the 15th century, nevertheless has its place among the major buildings of the Auvergne Romanesque school. As usual, its structure combines a triple nave, a "barlong" with tiered vaults and diaphragm-arches, whilst its capitals reflect the talent of a master craftsman who was working in about 1050. The fame of the church at Chauriat is due to its rich external decoration of mosaics, the polychromy of which sets off the paleness of the arkose, the reddish browns or dark ochres of the tuff and the grey black of the Volvic stone. Such mosaics which are found on a large number of churches in the Auvergne are not of Eastern origin but are a continuation of a Gallo-Roman tradition.

Saint-Martin de Cournon

The church at Cournon was extensively rebuilt recently. Those parts which date back to the mediaeval period are limited to the four bays of the nave, the diaphragm-arches of the transept crossing and part of the choir. This is enough to place the church among the major buildings of the regional school.

The chevet of Saint Austremoine at Issoire bathed in the morning sunlight.

Geometrical decorations.
Right, top, *Gemini, one of the signs of Zodiac on the chevet.*
Bottom - *Virgo and Libra, on the side chapel.*

SAINT AUSTREMOINE OR THE IDEAL ORDER

Henri Pourrat cleverly compared the church at Issoire to "certain old ladies who are better seen from the rear". Without dwelling on the pseudo-Romanesque front and bell towers, the visitor should see the apse and the transept, an architectural marvel, the harmony of which is the result of elaborate tiering and both subtle and rich decoration. Among the geometrical patterns of pale arkose, grey granite and black basalt which highlight this apse, the absidioles are decorated with remarkable sculptures representing the signs of the Zodiac, which start with Aries in the month of March, the beginning of the mediaeval year. In the 19th century the interior of the shrine was entirely painted and the recent restoration has revived these gaudy paintings. The 12th century made great use of such polychrome decorations, which made the capitals easier to interpret for pilgrims. These capitals are among the most famous in the Auvergne, in particular the very subtle composition which represents the Last Supper. On the other hand, the crypt with its ambulatory, which is one of the most successful of its type in the area, is totally bare and supported by eight, squat columns. It houses the Limoges enamelware reliquary, which contains the relics of Saint Austremoine.

The colonnade of the choir of the church of Saint Austremoine.
Right, top - *The capital of the Last Supper* ; bottom - *The Reliquary of Saint Austremoine.*

Below, left - *The Centaur capital, with its plant motifs* ; right - *The totally bare crypt.*

SAINT-SATURNIN, MAJOR MINIATURE

The shrines on the western edge of the Limagne, built on the model of the major churches on the plain, are of more modest dimensions - the church of Saint-Saturnin is half as long as the church at Issoire - but are built on exceptional sites. The church of Saint-Saturnin is built of arkose from Montpeyroux beside the castle of La Tour d'Auvergne, on a spur that separates the Monne from the Veyre. This building, which does not have radiating chapels or a narthex, has a beautifully mellowed octagonal bell tower, which is one of the rare examples to have survived the Revolution and which served as the model for most 19th century reconstructions.

Saint Saturnin.
Top - *The original bell-tower of Saint Saturnin.*
Opposite - *The choir and ambulatory of the church.*

The traditional mosaic cross of the South front.

Saint-Nectaire

Saint Nectaire, one of Saint Austremoine's companions, was one of the evangelists of the Basse Auvergne and the veneration that his tomb, on the Mont Cornadore, inspired explains the presence of a church in this unexpected location. This church, built of local, light grey trachyte stone, is not a major building by its dimensions or its rich decorations, for the apse is merely decorated with mosaic roses. On the other hand, its plan is that of a cathedral and the perfect harmony of its architecture and its natural setting make it a major building. Inside, the church of Saint-Nectaire is of faultless purity, with a perspective of columns rather than pillars, which leads worshippers towards the light of the choir. As is the custom, the six capitals of the apse recount with great success several episodes in the life of Christ and Saint Nectaire: in these boldly drawn scenes, there are no less than eighty-seven characters! The collection of relics and ornaments of Saint-Nectaire is famous for its Madonna in Glory and, above all, the bust reliquary of Saint Baudime, one of the patron saint's companions and to whom the mediaeval artist gave a fascinating face.

The magnificent order of Saint Nectaire.

The narthex of the church of Saint Nectaire.
Inset - *Notre-Dame du mont Cornadore, the Madonna in glory venerated under these arches.*

The capitals in the church at Saint-Nectaire include, from left to right, above: *The councillors, an episode from the life of Saint Nectaire, with the model of the church, and Christ in Hell accompanied by Adam and Eve.*
Centre - *The arrest of Christ, with Judas and the traitor's kiss, and Ranulfo, grasping a column, a capital which could be interpreted as a representation of the right of sanctuary;*
bottom - *The capital of the horseman of the Apocalypse the miracle of Saint Nectaire, brought back to life by the Pope and the archangel Saint Michael of the Last Judgement.*

Saint Baudime, an oak reliquary bust covered with repoussé-work copper and gilded leaves, which represent the companion of Saint Nectaire.
Inset - *Champlevé enamel book covers which also form part of the treasures of Saint Nectaire.*

Orcival, the Basilica of Our Lady

Of all the major Auvergnat churches, Notre-Dame of Orcival is the one that has best survived the centuries, in spiritual terms. The basilica of Orcival was built to house the highly venerated statue of a pilgrimage Madonna which still inspires the same fervour, eight hundred years later, at Ascensiontide and throughout the year. This very sober church is finished with grey andesite and phonolite roofing stones spotted with copper stains of lichen, and with its volumes cleverly arranged above the roofs of the village, it blends in perfectly with its mountain setting. Around the holy effigy, the choir of the basilica is a basket of light which sculpts the Romanesque curves, highlighting the work of the master masons. A single figured capital by the Master of Besse retraces the adventures of the money lender, as if to avoid attracting attention away from Our Lady, the only one in the region to have retained its facing of gold and silver. This Virgin with her "hands of light" was, for many years invoked by prisoners, as prove the chains hung ex-voto on the South transept.

The 12th century Our Lady of Orcival and the pilgrimage of the Ascension.

The perspective of the nave at Orcival.

Where the hammer falls

Why was the church of Orcival built on such a difficult site between the Sioulet, which had to be diverted and a mountain, which had to be excavated? It is said that following the discovery of the statue of the Virgin, which was to give rise to such devotion, every morning the masons responsible for building a new church on the site of an old chapel, on the hill of the "Tombeau", found their previous day's work demolished. To avoid going against the will of Heaven, the master builder threw his hammer and vowed to build the shrine where it fell, which was three hundred paces lower down, between the river and the stream...

The geometry of the golden section

The master builder of Notre-Dame-du-Port appears to have used the proportions of the golden section in the powerfully symbolic architecture of this shrine. It is a simple matter to show on a drawing that the nave without a narthex forms a golden rectangle, whilst with the narthex, it forms two squares the common side of which is highlighted by two columns, with no apparent useful purpose, engaged in the pillars. This layout is found at Orcival and Issoire. The ratio between the height of these columns and the width of the nave matches the golden section exactly and they also describe a perfect, smaller, rectangle on the narthex side. A study of the church as a whole reveals these proportions, to the nearest centimetre, in several places. Its geometry also uses Pythagoras' triangle and the corresponding angles that the workmen constructed with graduated lines to determine specific points, some of which are still marked with small wooden pegs.

Opposite - *The transept crossing of the basilica of Orcival with its diaphragm-arches, cupola on squinches and galleries.*
Inset - *The leg irons donated ex-voto, above the door of the transept.*

The Grande Limagne

From Arkose to Volvic Stone

"Une plaine infinie qui donnait aussitôt à l'âme la sensation d'un océan. Elle s'en allait, voilée d'une vapeur légère, une vapeur bleue et douce, cette plaine, jusqu'à des monts très lointains, à peine aperçus..." Black, heavy, thick, rich in silica and volcanic clays, since it is born of the mountains, the Limagne described by Maupassant is generous and this prosperous part of the Basse Auvergne was at the heart of the history of the province. Therefore, shrines gravitate around the major churches which were the source of Romanesque art in the Auvergne, thus reflecting the creative explosion in the Grande Limagne between the 10th and 12th centuries.

The Limagne near Moissat.
Inset - *The chevet of the church of Glaine-Montaigut.*

The "Hauts de Clermont"

The Church of Saint Pierre at Beaumont, which is a suburb of Clermont was part of a Benedictine abbey founded in 665. The building has the familiar plan of this order, with offset apses, whilst its pre-Romanesque nave was vaulted later during the 11th century with a transverse arch. The windows provide direct lighting, opening outwards under a trefoil arcade, which differentiates its church of Beaumont from the Limagne model. Chamalières, another suburb of Clermont, also owes the church of Notre-Dame to an old Benedictine collegiate church which was also vaulted later. Its nave and narthex are among the oldest in the province as the discovery of a silver denier with the head of Lothaire, who was king during the second half of the 10th century, proves. All that remains of the magnificent primitive apse, the harmony of which rivalled that of Notre-Dame-du-Port, is the crown of radiating chapels. Higher up, the church of Saint Léger at Royat paints a remarkable picture. Its castellated silhouette, from which rises the original turreted bell tower built of arkose only dating back to 1830, is nevertheless a sort of feudal armour which hides the truly Romanesque part of the shrine. The nave, preceded by a galleried narthex, dates back to the 11th century, whilst the transept, the flat chevet and the crypt were rebuilt in the 12th century.

Above - *The narthex of the church of Notre-Dame at Chamalières.*
Inset - *One of the capitals of the narthex.*
Below - *The "Maison de l'Eléphant" at Montferrand.*

The "Maison de l'Éléphant"

At Montferrand, which lies in the shadow of a southern Gothic church, Romanesque architecture is illustrated by the cellars of one of the oldest commanderies of the Knights Templar and the famous "Maison de l'Eléphant". Recently restored, this dwelling with its circular arches and characteristic columns is situated in the rue Kléber, formerly rue de la Saulnerie. It takes its name from the fresco of an elephant which decorates the arch of the central bay. It is assumed that this painting was commissioned by a merchant who had travelled in the East.

A DOOR FOR THE DEAD

The southern side of the church of Saint Léger at Royat has two small walled-up doors which opened out on to the cemetery next door. One of them, which is too low to walk through must have been a "door for the dead" used only to slide coffins into the cemetery after funeral services. This arrangement, which is very rare in Auvergne, can also be seen in the church at Messeix.

Above - *The church at Royat with the Puy de Dôme in the background.*
Below - *The oven-shaped vault at Beaumont with its transverse arches.*

At the edge of the puys

Volvic symbolises the relationships between the mountains and the Limagne plain through its church which combines lava and arkose. The only Romanesque part of the building is its chevet which is built of arkose, because in the 11th century techniques had not yet been developed to work the local stone. The side chapel, dedicated to Saint Priest, bishop of Clermont who was assassinated there in 764, has retained its original gate and houses a sword which is said to be that of the martyr. The columns of the chevet and ambulatory are decorated with several fine capitals. Not far away, the main claim to fame of the church of Marsat is its Romanesque Madonna, the vestments of which were gilded and the face painted black during the 19th century. This highly revered effigy is placed beside a curious "wax wheel" through which winds a never-ending candle, the fulfilment of a vow made to the Virgin in the 13th century.

Opposite - *The Madonna of Marsat, in walnut.*
Below - *Saint Priest at Volvic, with its typically Auvergnat plan.*

Churches of the Pays Brayaud

On the western edge of the Limagne we discover the rustic church of Saint Myon, still covered with roofing stones, like the great collegiate church of Saint Martin d'Artonne, which still has its original Romanesque choir gates. The church of the hamlet of La Chapelle at Vensat, which is built of warm Chaptuzat limestone, is remarkable for the harmony of its plan and its generous proportions. Finally, at Saint Hilaire-la-Croix, close to the limits of the province, we see decorations and sculptures which are inspired by Burgundy, for the fluted pilasters, the Guyenne for the trefoil tympanum door or by the Saintonge for its column swallowing monsters.

Top - *The choir of Saint Martin d'Artonne and the gates of the choir.*
Opposite - *The porch of the church of Saint Hilaire-la-Croix.*

ON THE BANKS OF THE ALLIER

The Romanesque shrines of the banks of the Allier, in the heart of the Grande Limagne, also illustrate the variety of the structural arrangements adopted by Auvergnat builders. Therefore, the church at Ris appears at first to have been very wide and square, and in the centre of which was later built a pointed arch nave, four times higher than wide.

The church of Luzillat, which dates back to the end of the Romanesque period, is typical of the Limagne, other than the fact that it does not have an ambulatory. It combines a blind nave with three bays, butressed by the vaults of the side aisles, a domed transept and a chevet with three apses.

On the other hand, Maringues has a large composite church, the ambulatory of which is the most interesting part. The capitals, the themes of which are typically Auvergnat, feature in particular a variation on the captive monkey, which is held on a lead by a horseman.

At Pont-du-Château, the church of Sainte-Martine opens out on to an impressive galleried narthex, the only purely Romanesque part of the building. The interesting original capitals were repainted under the Restoration by a priest who considered them too licentious...

Top - *Sainte-Martine of Pont-du-Château.*
Opposite - *The capital of Adam and Eve at Thuret.*

THURET, A CHURCH FOR THE INITIATED ?

Saved from a Benedictine priory owned by the abbey of Saint Alyre, the church of Saint Limin at Thuret has retained a series of sculpted capitals, from its first construction campaign during the 11th century, which still intrigue the experts. The usual local themes, such as the captive monkey, Adam and Eve, chalice griffins or the Good Shepherd are handled archaically, with little relief and are highly stylised, which highlights the polychromy. But we are also presented with unusual scenes, such as a wader which is devouring a snake or a strange wedding scene, which shows a vulgar woman behind whom is a demon's head, whose mouth is vomiting snakes. Faced with the false naïveté of these sculptures, made under the instruction of highly cultivated monks, the experts have raised the possibility that they contained messages for the initiated. The sculpture which caps the lintel of the South door and which represents a juggler doing a somersault holding a concave mirror in his hand, may be a clue to the special nature of this shrine.

Above - *One of the capitals at Maringues, Christ blessing a leper.*
Left - *The lantern of the dead at Culhat.*

Below - *The simple church of Culhat.*

The Lantern of the Dead at Culhat

Several regions have retained a Roman tradition according to which the living and the dead remained linked by means of a flame. For this, lanterns of the dead were built, they were sorts of lighthouses with a man-size opening to enable the lamp to be raised using a rope and pulley. This practice was common in cemeteries far from villages and during plague epidemics, to enable the flame to be collected without coming into contact with the neighbours. Only one of these structures from the Romanesque period remains in the Basse Auvergne, at Culhat. In the Cantal, several lanterns have been conserved, at Mauriac for example, but they are more recent reconstructions.

The Limagne and the "Buttes"

The charm of the countryside around Billom is such that is may be compared to Tuscany. The old churches are not the least of the charms of this southern part of the Grande Limagne. Although extensively remodelled in the Gothic style, the church of Saint Cerneuf at Billom still has its primitive choir and ambulatory, closed off by a remarkable 13th century cast iron gate. It has retained a superb 11th century crypt with four radiating chapels, an apse with eight columns, decorated with 12th century frescos, which is one of the most typical of the Auvergne.
Although simple, the church of the neighbouring village of Glaine-Montaigut is admirable for the beauty of the pale, veined arkose which gives its chevet amazingly warm colours. It shows the development of Romanesque art in the Auvergne, by combining a nave and primitive transept with this choir and apse, which are a triumph of the specific nature of the regional school.

Above left -*The church of Glaine-Montaigut the interior of which has been restored recently.*

Saint Austremoine at Lezoux

According to tradition and confirmed by the discovery of potery shards signed by Stremonius, the future Saint Austremoine left Rome to convert the Auvergne and stopped off in the pottery town of Lezoux where he practised his trade for long enough to gather some disciples. These included Claudia, Gerlène her niece and a Roman soldier called Fabius, who was torn to pieces by a mob whilst defending Claudia's house, where Christians gathered in secret and Gerlène died of a broken heart. Legend has it that the lovers were buried side by side, which is perhaps true since, during the 19th century, the remains of a young woman next to those of a man with the remains of armour and a fibula were exhumed. In addition, the town has an ancient 11th century Romanesque church dedicated to Saint Austremoine that has a crypt: could this be the cellar of Claudia's house where the first of the Auvergnat faithful worshipped?

The ex-voto of watermen

Beauregard-l'Evêque, which was the summer residence of the bishops of Clermont, on the banks of the Allier, still has in the middle of a cemetery, its ancient primitive Romanesque church of Saint Aventin. This was the fording point for the old road between Clermont and Thiers, and a small port for the watermen who came down the Allier. The chapel of Saint Aventin, which is one of the oldest churches in the Auvergne, recalls this period in the form a boat suspended from the nave.

Above - *The 12th century gates of the choir at Billom.*
Below - *The crypt of the church of Saint Cerneuf at Billom, which has never been changed, is a model of early Romanesque art in the Auvergne.*

The Limagne and the Bourbonnais Mountains

Under Burgundian influence

In days gone by, the Bourbonnais was subject to many influences, from the Auvergne in particular, but also from the Berry, the Nivernais and Burgundy, as shown by the limit between the langue d'oil (future French) and langue d'oc (Provençal) and the change from roofs of flat tiles to round tiles. From the 11th century on, the Bourbons drew their power from the break up of the country. In terms of Romanesque art, the southern part of the region included in part within of the former diocese of the Auvergne, at the cross roads of various artistic movements.

The church of Saint Julien de Meillers and the horizon of the Bourbonnais.
Inset - *The church of Saint Laurent de Châtel-de-Neuvre and its primitive nave.*

From the mountains to the Allier

To the east, a special Romanesque monument is built on the Bourbonnais Limagne surrounded by mountains. The church of Châtel-Montagne is a building of rough granite which combines the traditions of the Auvergne and a three tier arrangement inspired by Cluny. Later, a decorated West front, an unusual feature for this area, was added to this majestic church. Situated in the middle of the plain beyond the Allier, the church of Biozat is typical of the Limagne, with capitals on themes similar to those seen at Mozac. Close by, Gannat has two churches that are completely or partially Romanesque belonging to Issoire abbey. But the claim to fame of the town may be found in its castle museum: it is a 12th century Evangelary from Ebreuil, mounted with a Carolingian ivory plaque representing the Crucifixion and the Resurrection.

The front of the church of Châtel-Montagne, which was added later.
Below - *The capital of the pack mule.*

Humour in granite

The sculptors of the church of Châtel-Montagne did not allow themselves to be discouraged by the coarse grained granite they had at their disposal. They saw the funny side, as may be seen by examining the capitals of the shrine. These delightful compositions feature quadrupeds on their hind legs biting their tails, busts of men blowing ivory horns, a mermaid or monkey-headed atlantes. A humorous capital represents an obstinate donkey laden with a pack, pulled by a man at the front, whilst his companion is braced against the rear end of the animal, a radical means of getting it to move, it would appear.

The Gannat Evangelary.
Top left - *Saint Mark and his lion.*
Right - *The ivory binding board.*

Bottom left - *Illuminations:*
Right - *Saint Matthew and his symbolic creature.*
Centre - *The cover decorated with enamelware and precious stones.*

A REFUGE ON THE BANKS OF THE SIOULE

Ebreuil entered history when Louis the Pious, the son of Charlemagne, made it his winter palace. The spiritual role of the place was confirmed in 898, when monks from Saint-Maixent-en-Poitou, fleeing the Normans, came to shelter the relics of Saint Léger. A Benedictine abbey was built and the present church was part of it. Behind a 12th century porch bell tower, the framed nave and the transept of the building date back to the very first Romanesque period in the Auvergne. The gallery of the nave is covered by one of the most important cycles of Romanesque paintings in the province, and which is devoted to Saint Austremoine, Saint Pancras and Saint Valérie in particular. Nearby is the ancient priory of Ebreuil dedicated to Saint Saturnin.

The church of Veauce in the morning sunlight.
Below, left - *At Veauce, the high ambulatory and choir.*

ANIMAL SKINS AND LIONS' SNOUTS

The church of Saint Léger at Ebreuil retains its early 12th century doors, the metal work of which was much admired by Viollet-the-Duc.
"Chaque vantail n'est suspendu que par deux pentures ; sept fausses pentures garnissent les frises et les maintiennent entre elles. La fausse penture du milieu, plus riche que les six autres, forme une double palmette d'un beau caractère. Ces ferrures sont posées sur des peaux marouflées sur le bois et peintes en rouge vif."
They would have been bear skins like those at Orcival. Like the church of Saint Julien at Brioude, this door also has two bronze knockers decorated with stylised lions' heads. One of them is marked with the Latin inscription ADEST PORTA PER QUAM JUSTI REDEUNT AD PATRIAM: *here is the door through which the just return to their homeland.*

The ancient church of Saint-Léger at Ebreuil, preceded by its elegant porch bell-tower.

Below, left - *One of the bronze knockers of the church of Saint Léger.*
Right, top - *The fresco of the Annunciation, with the Virgin Mary with open arms, wearing a veil.*
Bottom - *The fresco of the martyrdom of Saint Valérie: Étienne, her fiancé holds out the sword for the executioner.*

Souvigny, the jewel of the Ile de Bourbon

The term "Ile de Bourbon" refers to the small region between Moulins, Souvigny and Bourbon-l'Archambault, where the history of the Bourbonnais was played out and which contains most of the province's major monuments. The church of Saint-Pierre at Souvigny has the richest heritage of this area. This pilgrimage shrine which could accommodate ten to twelve thousand worshippers has been altered many times over the centuries, but it has retained a largely Romanesque nave and chevet inspired by that of Issoire. The places that depended on Souvigny include Châtel-de-Neuvre on a magnificent site overlooking the Allier. This austere church, whose purity of style is remarkable, is a wonderful example of early Romanesque art.

The "Tomb of Saint Mayeul"

It was thanks to two holy abbots of Cluny, who died within its walls, that Souvigny abbey became the most beautiful shrine in the Bourbonnais and the burial place of the Dukes of Bourbon. The story began in 916 when Aymard, one of the ancestors of the Bourbons, left his property in Souvigny to Cluny abbey. Mayeul de Provence, the fourth abbot of Cluny, died in 994 at Souvigny, during one of his trips and is buried there. He was canonised immediately and his tomb attracted thousands of pilgrims, including Hugues Capet. His successor, Odilon de Mercœur, started the construction of the present church and developed the Cluny order considerably and became enormously popular by introducing the "Truce of God". He died in 1049 at Souvigny and was also canonised. He lies beside Saint Mayeul in a remarkable, finely sculpted Romanesque tomb behind the left entrance door.

The Romanesque-Burgundian aisle of the priory with the tomb of Saint Mayeul.

The Romanesque Souvigny "Calendar"

Opposite the large priory church of Souvigny, lies the ancient church of Saint-Marc, a building in the Romanesque Burgundian style and which has recently been converted into a museum of sculpture. It is in this context that the most remarkable item of the Abbey's heritage is displayed; the famous Romanesque "calendar". It is also known as the "pillar", "octagon" or "column of the Zodiac", reflecting the difficulty experts have with it. This piece is a solid octagonal pillar weighing some 840 kg, as high as a man and obviously has more than half missing. One side of this column is sculpted to represent the months of the year, the signs of the Zodiac, fabulous beings and fantastic or exotic animals.

The series of months shows, in particular, peasants threshing grain with a flail, a vine grower treading grapes that another is pouring into the vat and a frugal winter meal. Among the signs of the Zodiac, one notes a strange, four-legged creature with a pointed tail and which is supposed to represent Scorpio. The fantastic animals include a mermaid and a four-legged animal with a human head. The space between these two sculpted faces is richly decorated with Greek key-patterns, foliated scrolls and bands of tracery and palmettes which enable the work to be dated to the end of the 12th century. It is generally thought that this "pillar" was used to hold candles at Easter.

On the calendar, working in the fields.
Top left - *12th century silver coins.*

The chevet of the monumental church of Saint Menoux.
Opposite - *The choir and its apse with seven columns with their wonderful capitals.*
Inset - *The famous "débredinoire" a sarcophagus of its patron Saint with an opening in its side through which the simple minded, the "bredins" in this part of the country, poked their heads in the hope of being cured.*

ON THE EDGE OF THE AUVERGNE

To the north of the former diocese of Clermont, Auvergnat Romanesque art has been emulated, both in terms of architecture and statuary. Therefore, in the church of Saint Georges de Bourbon-l'Archambault, one may differentiate between what is inspired by Souvigny, and therefore indirectly by Cluny, and what is purely Auvergnat tradition. The influence of Burgundy is particularly noticeable in the decorative details, whilst the Auvergne is present in the form of splendid capitals. The church of the Sainte-Trinité (Holy Trinity) Autry-Issards has one of the finest examples of regional sculpture, in the sculpted door lintel. This work is very rare in that it bears the name of its creator, identified by the inscription NATALIS ME FE(cit). This saddle-back lintel is decorated with a mandorla, from which the figure of Christ has unfortunately disappeared, showing the archangels Michael and Gabriel, in a tableau which betrays its Auvergnat influences from the door of the church of Sainte-Foy at Conques. For further confirmation, one merely needs to go to Neuilly-en-Donjon in the eastern fringes of the Bourbonnais, where the door of the church is decorated with a lintel inspired by the Burgundian school. This highly raised sculpture represents the Adoration of the Magi, Adam and Eve and the Last Supper. Montluçon reveals how Romanesque art in the Auvergne was able to be combined with ideas from the nearby Berry. The church of Saint-Pierre, which depended on the archbishop of Huriel, combines a perfectly Auvergnat cupola on squinches with typical "passages berrichons" which link a nave without aisles to the arms of the transept. Within a stone's throw from Montluçon, the church of Saint Georges at Néris-les-Bains, shows the influence of the Auvergnat tradition with its chevet and ambulatory and three radiating chapels, capped with gables, which remind us of Saint Nectaire.

Above - *The Burgundian door of Neuilly-en-Donjon. The lintel representing the Last Supper shows Mary Magdalene at the feet of Christ.*

Opposite, top - *The church of Bourbon-l'Archambault and the Musicians' capital.*
Bottom - *The door of the church of Autry-Issards and a detail of the lintel.*

Below, left - *The church of Saint Pierre at Montluçon with its narrow "passages berrichons" at the sides.* Right - *The church of Néris-les-Bains.*

More important, the church of Saint Vincent de Chantelle which is built within the walls of the château of the Dukes of Bourbon is no less representative of the regional model with its superb tiered chevet. Its capitals include one showing two leaping animals and curious human masks.

The flamboyant Gothic Cathedral of Notre-Dame in Moulins, the prosperous capital of the Dukes of Bourbon, retains a reminder of the Romanesque period in the form of a Black Madonna in the Auvergnat style, similar to the one at Le Puy. Nearby, the church of Meillers houses a moving Virgin and Child, the features of which appear to be those of a local peasant woman. The portal of this Bourbon bocage village church has a superb saddle-back lintel typical of the region.

Until the Hundred Years War, Yzeure remained the seat of the parish of Moulins, of which it is now a suburb. The Romanesque church of Yzeure depended on the diocese of Autun and it is no surprise to find Burgundian ornamentation similar to that of Souvigny. The affiliation of a church was highlighted whenever possible, hence the church at Le Montet, which depended on an abbey in the Piedmont, shows signs of Italian Romanesque architecture.

Top, left - *The capital of the musical ass and lion at Meillers.*
Top, right - *The Church of Saint Julien at Meillers with its "barlong" bell-tower.*
Bottom, left - *The Madonna of Meillers.* Right - *The tympanum of the church of Meillers.*

The church of Chantelle.
Below, left - *The door at Le Montet.* Right - *The 12th century Black Madonna of Moulins.*

The church of Agonges with its Burgundian decoration.

The bell-tower of the church at Franchesse.

The Romanesque buildings of the Limagne plain in the Bourbonnais have certain resemblances: the bell tower of the church of Agonges, to the north of Saint Menoux, reminds us of those at Meillers or Saint Léger d'Ebreuil with its rectangular ground plan, as does the bell tower of the church of Saint Étienne de Franchesse. On the other hand, the 11th and 12th century bell tower of the church of Saint Martin of Coulandon is a square tower, only the base of which is a barlong.

The church of Coulandon, with its typically Bourbonnais gossip-chair.

The church of Yzeure
Above - *This 12th century building has a Burgundian door-way with a bare tympanum.*

Right - *The bell-tower is a square tower on an 18th century balustrade.*

Bottom - *Above the door-way there are many varied and expressive modillions.*

Livradois, Comté and Dauphiné

In and around the valleys of the Dore and Allier

From the "Pays de Thiers" to La Chaise-Dieu, the Dore has eroded a deep gash in the Monts d'Auvergne, towards the Velay. To the east of this river, rises the barrier of the Monts du Forez, a desert-like end to the Auvergne. On the other side, runs the soft swell of the Monts du Livradois, another land of grass and woods, better suited to human enterprise. This region, the praises of which have been sung by Henri Pourrat extends into the historic entities: the Comté and the Dauphiné d'Auvergne, areas studded with volcanic buttes on both sides of the Allier valley. During the 12th century, these hills were covered with generally simple churches of remarkable diversity. Some of their architectural features come from the Velay or the Forez, whilst their decoration is Auvergnat. Furthermore, the variety of the structural arrangements adopted stems from the fact that many of these churches were priories or collegiate churches that depended on several important abbeys: Manglieu, Issoire, Sauxillanges and above all La Chaise-Dieu.During the Gothic period, when La Chaise-Dieu adopted the new style, many churches in the Livradois and the Comté were also brought up to date.

The Dore valley in the early morning sunlight.
Inset - *Detail of the portal of the church of Saint Dier d'Auvergne.*

The largest cupola in the Auvergne in the church of Saint Genès in Thiers. Below - The exubérance and naïveté of the capitals at Le Moûtiers.

Two churches on the Durolle

Saint Avit, bishop of Clermont, gave Thiers its first church dedicated to Saint Genès, built on the plateau at the end of the 6th century, whilst a little later, the town saw a Benedictine abbey rise and prosper in its lower quarters, which retained the name of Le Moûtier. The two Romanesque churches in the capital of the cutlery industry are their heirs. Saint Genès has the widest nave in the Auvergne, and originally had a wooden roof. The transept crossing is topped with a cupola to rival the nave, a rare example of the audacity of the local master builders. The recent restoration of the church revealed a fine 12th century fresco of Christ giving his blessing in the apse, together with fragments of mosaic from the Merovingian church. The church of Le Moûtiers, which was disfigured by its restoration in 1882, retains its 12th century capitals, on which regional symbolism is tinged with antique influences.

The church of Saint Genès at Thiers. Above - *The fresco of Christ giving his blessing.*

WORKING OUR WAY BACK UP THE DORE

Further up the Dore, Courpière shares its expertise in cutlery with Thiers and its Romanesque church with capitals signed by the Maître du Moûtiers. Then come Arlanc and Dore-l'Eglise. The first is built around a church with three naves and three bays capped by a Gothic bell tower, whilst the shrine of the second has a front with a long staircase.

WHAT IS THIS BALL?

The capitals in the church of Courpière are both original and well executed. One of them shows two running figures holding large balls in their hands. Are they children playing ball, a forerunner of the modern game of boules or some forgotten symbol?

DIVINE PUNISHMENT STRIKES THE LORD OF BELLE-FILLE

The church of Dore-l'Eglise opens with doors on picturesque 13th century hinges. In the surrounding area, it is said that they come from the now lost castle of Belle-Fille, the Lord of which had a very high opinion of his prerogatives. It was forbidden to start mass without him. One day, when the Lord of the manor was excessively late, the priest decided to start proceedings. When he finally arrived and saw that the service had started, the wretched character leaped on the priest and stabbed him to death. At that very instant, the murderer was struck by lighting and another bolt burned down his castle; all that was left were the doors, which were miraculously intact and which the daughter of the Lord of the manor had brought to the church.

The church of Arlanc and the village. Below - *The chevet and the trefoil apse of the church of Arlanc.*

Opposite, top - *The portal of the church at Dore-l'Eglise.* Bottom - *One of its Romanesque door leaves.* Centre - *The strange capital at Courpière.*

Above, left - *The church of Ronzières.*
Right - *A blind arcade of the church at Mailhat.* Inset - *An overall view of the shrine.*
Below - *The narthex of the church of Saint Sébastien at Manglieu.*

The apple tree which became Manglieu

In about 630, Magnus, an old Auvergnat monk who was very ill, went to Rome to pray at the tomb of Saint Sebastian and was cured. When he returned home with a relic of his saviour, he spent the last night of his trip under a local apple tree, on which he had hung his precious cargo. But in the morning, the branch on which he had hung his bag was out of reach and several people called upon to help had their health restored before this tree. Clearly the relics had to stay, and Saint Genès, the bishop of Clermont, founded one of the oldest monasteries of the province at the foot of the miraculous tree. The place was named the place of Magnus, Magnilocensi, which became Manglieu.

The church of Colamine-sous-Vodable.

Square bell-towers in the region of the "Buttes"

In the countryside between the Dore and the Allier, we find the church of Saint Dier, the former priory of La Chaise-Dieu abbey which, as often in the Velay has a front with a portal with polychrome voussoirs, and the curious abbey church of Manglieu, which retains a Romanesque narthex with two stories and a Merovingian chevet. The simple church of Mailhat belongs to the archaic family of buildings with a single nave, with an apse with side chapels built into the wall. Finally, the church of Ronzières, an original composite building dedicated to Saint Baudime must be seen. Pilgrims came here to revere a Romanesque Madonna of painted wood, whose face is astonishingly pure.

The chevet of the church of Saint Dier, Left -*Velay style door.*

The "Pays de la Haute Sioule"

The Combraille in the Auvergne – since this region, without a capital, extends into the Creuse and Bourbonnais- is a patchwork that rivers and in particular the Sioule have carved into deep valleys. In the early days of Christianity, hermits found refuges ideal for contemplation and prayer and which became influential abbeys, such as Menat and Montfermy. To the south, lies the harsh landscape of the volcanoes. At the foot of these mountains, religious fervour was no less durable, as prove the crowds that gather for the pilgrimage to the church of Orcival or who follow Notre-Dame de Vassivière in her peregrinations. Madonnas in Glory also watch over Vergheas, Comps and Heume-l'Eglise, the shrines of which are at least partially Romanesque.

The church of Saint Léger de Montfermy overlooking the Sioule.
Inset - *The Madonna of Heume-l'Eglise, who watches over the villages behind the door of the church.*

FROM THE COMBRAILLE TO THE MONTS DORE

Top - *The church of Saint Fargeon at Bourg-Lastic.*
Bottom - *The vast three nave church at Menat.*

The church of Miremont, near Le Sioulet.

The beginnings of Romanesque sculpture

Romanesque sculpture emerged in about the year 1000, mainly on portals and their tympana, which the Auvergnat tradition often set aside in favour of the decoration of saddle-back lintels. Nevertheless, it is through the capitals of its shrines that the region best reflects the personality of its "image makers". If we have to name the oldest examples of sculpture passed down to us from this period, it is without doubt those found in the church of Biollet. The shrine itself, which is built of fine pale granite, is primitive in appearance, with pillars which are too strong for the vaults they support, transverse arches which are not common in the area and a narrow choir which could be Carolingian. And what can be said of the "barbaric" capitals which decorate this church? The capitals at Biollet represent strange animals and embryonic, sometimes entwined figures, who are often holding a small cross in their hands. This stylisation of the figures, together with the absence of relief, probably means that the Gallic influence was still strong in the Auvergne of the year 1000.

In granite and slate

On the edge of the middle Sioule, which forms a graceful meander here, the remains of the Carthusian monastery of Port-Sainte-Mary, lost in a wild location, conjure up the beginnings of Christianity. Close by, on the site of the hermitage of Saint Brachio, the church of Saint Léger at Montfermy has a harmonious trefoil chevet and admirable capitals sculpted by a pupil of the Master of Mozac. In the outer reaches of the region, the closeness of the Limousin is higtlighted in the church of Herment by a cupola on pendentives and at Bourg-Lastic by the discrete nature of the sculpted capitals.

Celtic reminders

The village of Saint Ours, close to Montfermy, still has a Romanesque chapel dedicated to the local patron, Saint Ours, who was a follower of Saint Victor and remains a mysterious figure. His name could be the Christian form of Orcus, the god of the underworld, an ogre in animal form, and after which Orcival and Orcet may also have been named.

A primitive capital at Biollet.

The fresco showing the construction of the church of Montfermy.

The austere church of Herment (Puy-de-Dôme).
Below - *The polygonal chevet at Meymac (Corrèze).*
Right - *At Meymac, a bishop and a worshipper on his knees... monsters devouring women.*

Limousin, a Land of Saints

The Limousin was also one of the great centres of monasticism in the region. Here, Romanesque art, close to that of the Auvergne, was developed by the religious orders which filled their horizons with these hexagonal bell towers with square bases, so characteristic of the province. The other originality of the Limousin is the almost exclusive use of granite, which is not very suitable for sculpture and which gives the shrines a "Cistercian" austerity. The province adopted discoveries from neighbouring areas and, in particular the technique of the vaulted nave buttressed by means of the quadrant vaulted aisles or galleries, developed by the builders in the Auvergne.

The abbey church of Meymac contains some of these architectural borrowings, but it is due to its Holy Black Madonna that the shrine is closest to the churches of the neighbouring province. Despite this, the 12th century wooden effigy is quite unique, since the artist who made it carved it with a "turban" on its head.

The Virgin "with the turban" at Meymac, also known as "the Egyptian".
Below - *The apses at Meymac, which are curved inside under a half cupola.*

Beaulieu, at the crossroads of the Romanesque routes

During the Middle Ages, the major centres of pilgrimage played an essential role in the human and cultural melting pot and Beaulieu-sur-Dordogne is a perfect example. Beaulieu, close to Rocamadour and which was famous for the relics it housed, was at the crossroads of the routes leading to the Aquitaine, the Auvergne and Conques, and from Saint Martial at Limoges to Saint Cernin in Toulouse via Cahors and Moissac. Pilgrims streamed towards the abbey church of Saint Pierre, whose architecture symbolises the meeting of the Limousin, Auvergnat and Quercy schools.

This Romanesque yellow sandstone building built by the monks of Cluny only contains discreet sculpture decorations. On the other hand, the image makers from Toulouse, who exercised their talents at Collonges-la-Rouge, Moissac and Souillac, gave it its Southern porch, which is a jewel of Romanesque sculpture. The tympanum and lintel represent the Last Judgement and show Heaven, Earth and Hell, in a powerful evocation of Christ impassive with his arms outstretched. The freedom of the composition and the care taken with the details show that this work is of the Languedoc school.

Below, left - *The perfectly constructed choir of the abbey church at Beaulieu (Corrèze).*
The Adoration of the Magi on the 13th century Beaulieu reliquary, copper champlevé enamel work.

Overall view of the portal at Beaulieu. Left - *A detail representing the three temptations of Christ.*

Below - *The Madonna of Beaulieu, from the early Gothic period, is still slightly Romanesque. To the right of the central pier, an old man who may be Isiah.*

In Lava and Roofing Stones

The church of Chambon-sur-Lac, close to the summits of the massif du Sancy, owes its squat appearance to the fact that the ground level was raised up after each flood of the Couze de Chaudefour. Note the saddle-back lintel of the porch which represents the Stoning of Saint Étienne, the local patron Saint. The stone roofs of Besse-en-Chandesse, a charming Renaissance town, the prosperity of which is due to the production of cheese, cluster around the church of Saint André. The mountain character of this shrine is revealed by its squat proportions and the coarse treatment of its figured capitals. Close inspection of these sculptures in volcanic stone reveals Saint André in torment on a Latin cross and a man with a wooden leg leading a strange sacrifice scene. But, the Bessards (the people of Besse) only have eyes for the statue of Notre-Dame-de-Vassivière, at least when their Virgin is not in her mountain chapel, in the middle of their herds in summer pasture.

The baptistery at Chambon-sur-Lac.
Inset - *Exterior capitals.*

An Enigmatic Capital

At Chambon-sur-Lac, on the slope to which the cemetery was moved, stands an original Romanesque building, referred to as the rotunda or baptistery. The primitive purpose of this shrine is not clear, tradition has it that it was the mausoleum of the Lords of Murol. Questions have been raised concerning one of the capitals of the building, which shows a man naked, lying in a bed, surrounded by figures who are taking great interest in him. Does this scene represent the circumcision of Abraham, as is generally thought, the martyrdom of a Saint or an evocation of traditional medical practices? Some consider that the capital is a reference to a pagan castration ceremony, since one of the figures who is dressed in the oriental style, appears to be wearing the insignia of the cult of Cybele. The capitals of the external columns show a figure who could be Attis, Cybele's lover, which would confirm this hypothesis.

Besse-en-Chandesse (Puy-de-Dôme).

Below - *The capitals of the church of Saint-André :* left - *The sacrifice by the man with a wooden leg.* Centre - *The torment of Saint André.* Right - *The feast of the Dives.*

On the 2nd July, for one of the most popular pilgrimages in the Auvergne, Notre-Dame de Vassivière leaves the church of Besse to be carried up to her mountain chapel.
Inset - *The Black Madonna.*

An inventory of capitals

On the capitals of Auvergnat churches, the sculptors of the Romanesque period gave the best of their art, taking their inspiration from a wide range of sources. The region retained Gallo-Roman influences, hence a thick-set character clothed in generous draped garments. Many subjects are taken from Antiquity but biblical and evangelical themes are also common, as are the lives of the saints. The province was also inspired by oriental fabrics, hence birds with tails in the form of foliage, many lions with two bodies and the two-headed eagles at Saint Germain-l'Herm. The Middle Ages also liked fabulous animals and symbolic figures, including the "captive monkey", the money lender, the musical ass and the billy goat with a rider, which condemn, evil, greed, foolishness and lust, respectively. Finally, a few rare capitals pay homage to benefactors, as at Volvic with Guillaume de Bezac and Notre-Dame-du-Port with Stephanus.

Above - *The fresco of the denial of Saint Pierre.* Below - *The cave chapel at Jonas.*

Do not leave the region without visiting the astonishing troglodyte village of Jonas, further down the couze Pavin. This tuff cliff which has been excavated on several stories, contains an original Romanesque chapel, decorated with 11th century frescoes, which are the oldest in the Auvergne.

The Region of Wall Belfries

The Haute Auvergne, which corresponds to the department of the Cantal, lies around the great volcanic massif of the same name, in which rivers have eroded deep valleys. Although pastoral farming has been carried out on the upper slopes for many generations, the difficulties due to altitude have meant that human occupation is concentrated in the valleys. In the Romanesque period, no town had been developed in the Haute Auvergne, where only abbeys had been established: the monastery of Aurillac was founded in the 9th century by Saint Géraud, several decades after the priory of Mauriac and a century before the primitive abbey church of Saint Flour. The last great monastic church was built at Montsalvy in about 1070.

The valley of the Allagnon, the gateway to the Cantal, watched over by the chapel Sainte-Madeleine.
Inset - *The chapel and its stone roof.*

Reminder of a Prehistoric Religion

In days gone by, two chapels, one dedicated to Saint Victor and the other to Sainte Madeleine, stood on the basalt cliffs which face each other between Blesle and Massiac. Legend has it that these two Saints met to pray in the middle of the valley, on the rosary that Sainte Madeleine changed into a footbridge. All that remains is the 11th century chapel which succeeded the oratory to the Saint, on the edge of the cliff, above a cave which appears to be a sacred place dating back to the mists of time. On their return from the annual pilgrimage, which is still followed, to the chapel Sainte-Madeleine on the 22nd July, the Saint's day, pilgrims never fail to place flowers in this cave, which has been sacred since the time of the standing stones.

The Haute-Auvergne

Beside the abbey churches of Mauriac and Montsalvy which have come down to us through the ages, more modest conventual churches remain. Their fame is often due to a picturesque location, for example Bredons, Brageac or Vignonet. Romanesque architecture may also be seen in simple, country shrines with stone roofs and a characteristic wall belfry, which sometimes house an inspiring Madonna in Glory.

Top - *The mountain church of Chastel-sur-Murat, reminiscent of a buron (sheep barn), with its communal oven.*
Left - *The church of Allanche, which has been fortified.*

The glories of the Allagnon

The valley of the Allagnon has two Romanesque landmarks of unequalled reputation; the chapel of Vauclair, nestling in the bottom of the gorge and which is vaguely Limousin in appearance. Every 8th September, pilgrims gather before one of the most magnificent Madonnas in the province. This fascinating statue shows Mary dressed in an elegantly draped tunic, with her head slightly bowed, giving her an extraordinary gentleness, carrying the Infant Jesus who has a hieratic expression. Like other reliquary statues, this Madonna has a rock crystal cabochon, through which the relics she contains are visible.

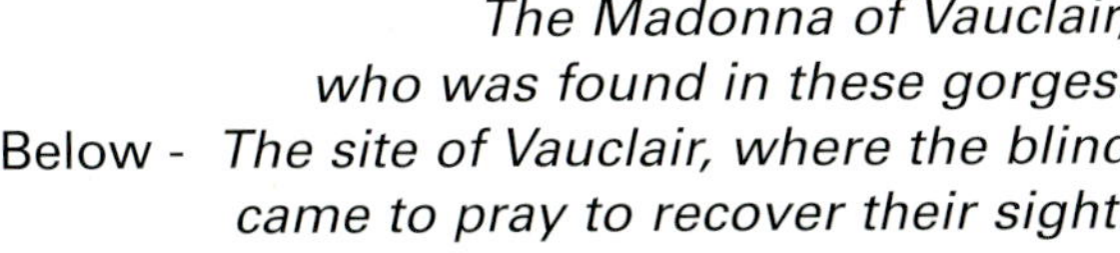

The Madonna of Vauclair, who was found in these gorges.

Below - *The site of Vauclair, where the blind came to pray to recover their sight.*

Murat and the Bredons priory.

Up river, the church of Bredons attracts all the attention, alone on the top of an enormous volcanic neck that dominates the town of Murat. It was part of the priory of Moissac founded in about 1050, as can be seen by the fine drafting of its basalt stones and its southern porch with triple recessed orders. For generations, the church of Bredons hid a statue of its patron Saint Pierre, which is one of the jewels of Romanesque art.

The key of Saint Pierre to the rescue of the rabid

The church of Saint-Pierre at Bredons has a studded door, the key of which was used for a curious purpose for many years: it was heated until red hot and used to cauterise the bites of rabid dogs.

The porch at Bredons. Right, top - *A capital with a plant motif.* Bottom - *One of the heads of the brackets of the columns in the choir.*

TWO CENTURIES OF OBSCURITY FOR SAINT PIERRE

The jewel of the decoration of the church of Saint Pierre at Bredons is one of its altarpieces, which stands on the high altar. When this monumental work was installed in about 1720, it masked a bay in which a niche housed an ancient statue of Saint Pierre. The curate decided to destroy this "barbaric" statue but, as he handled it, he discovered a small door in its back, behind which he found the relics of the patron Saint of the church: "Six, large and small bones wrapped in three linen cloths and yellow cloths bound with the same thread" in addition, the tonsure of the Saint concealed the cover of a second relic holder. The curate returned the statue to the niche with a note explaining its discovery and this precious Romanesque effigy of Saint Pierre was plunged into darkness behind the altarpiece. It was only rediscovered in 1954 and this polychrome work of art is now on display in the museum of Saint Flour.

The statue of Saint Pierre who should be holding keys in his hand.

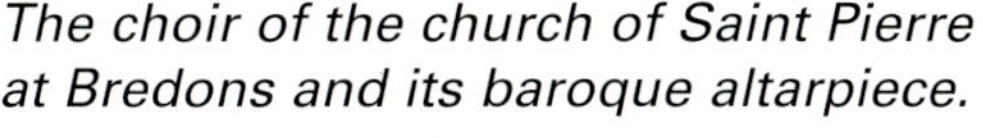

The choir of the church of Saint Pierre at Bredons and its baroque altarpiece.

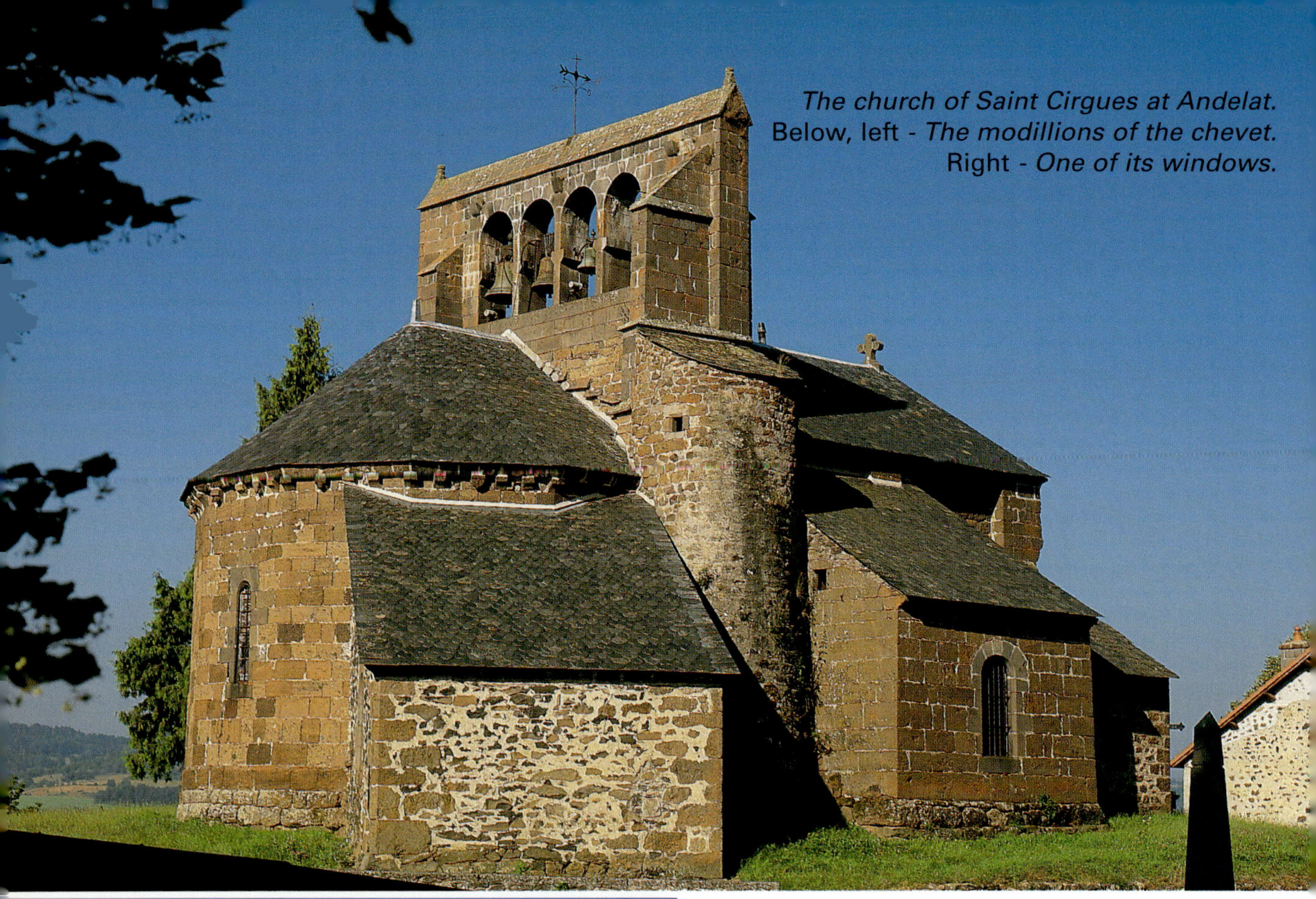

The church of Saint Cirgues at Andelat.
Below, left - *The modillions of the chevet.*
Right - *One of its windows.*

All bells to the wind on the Planèze

The Planèze of the Cantal, around Saint Flour, was often devastated, particularly during the Hundred Years War.
Compared by Henri Pourrat to a "Beauce rude et nue sous la bise passant et les grolles croassant", this land is therefore not very well endowed with shrines from the Romanesque period, which makes the typically Cantal churches of Andelat and Roffiac all the more precious. They are topped with large wall belfries with four arcades over a triumphal arch at the end of the nave. More unusually, they have a chevet which is hipped outside and semi-circular inside, with niche chapels built into the wall.

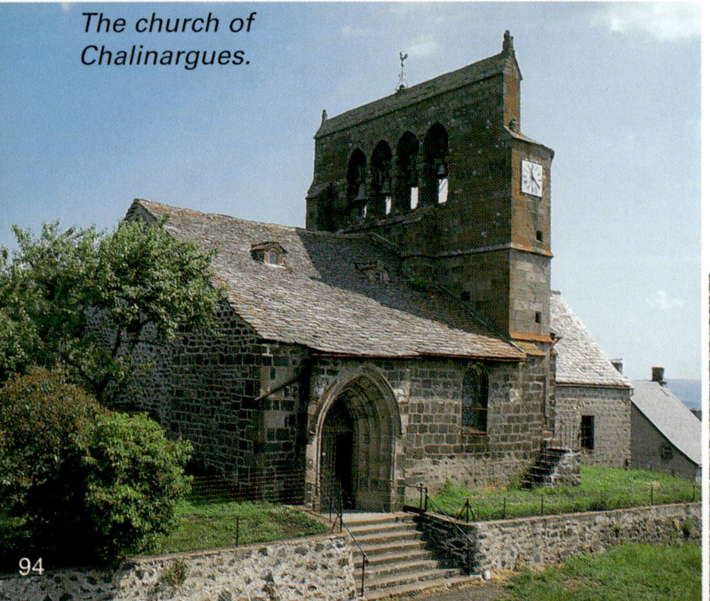

The church of Chalinargues.

Right - *The church of Roffiac.*
Left - *A capital on the chevet.*

The Black Christ

The only black Christ in France, the "Beau Dieu noir" in the Cathedral de Saint Flour hangs on the pillar to the left of the entrance of the choir. This life-size 13th century statue, the origin of which is unknown, is admirable for its harmony, the face of Christ has an expression of majesty and unequalled serene compassion. It was towards the middle of the 19th century that, for some unknown reason, the primitive polychromy of the statue was hidden under a uniform, black coating.

Top, right - *The church of Saint Hippolyte, at the start of the pilgrimage to Font-Sainte.*
ITop, left - *The mountain church of Dienne.*
Above - *The capital of Lust at Dienne.*

ON THE MOUNTAIN OF THE BURONS

The harshness of the region is reflected in the squat architecture of the Romanesque mountain churches of the Cantal between Murat and Mauriac, their use of austere volcanic rock, their sober decoration and blind front, since the portal opens out to the south and is often protected by a porch or deep recess. Their model could be the church of Dienne, which has as its backdrop the highest mountains of the region with their slopes strewn with basaltic rock, and which houses a wooden Romanesque Christ. In these mountains, the rites themselves often correspond to the ancestral way of life, as may be seen at La Font-Sainte, where the shepherds' Madonna "goes up" with the herds to the summer pastures and "comes down" in mid-October, to spend the winter in the church of Saint Hippolyte. Riom-ès-Mountains, a small local capital, grew up around an abbey, of which the church of Saint Georges remains. This typically Cantal building, was transformed by a turreted bell tower. The choir is decorated by capitals, some of which represent strange horsemen with archaic shields.

The church of Cheylade, which still has a choir, an apse and absidioles dating back to the Romanesque period.

The 12th century bourrée

Four of the capitals in the church at Menet represent interesting dance scenes from the Romanesque period. On the one hand, we can see women in dresses pirouetting with flying tresses and bearded men wearing skirts, which remind us of the Scottish kilt. Some have their arms raised whilst others have their hands on their hips, which is evocative of a popular dance, based on the Auvergnat bourrée. Furthermore, the men who are carrying square objects appear to be occupied with a more martial exercise, which could be some kind of war dance. One of these men, perhaps a master mason, is wearing an apron decorated with a star, over his kilt.

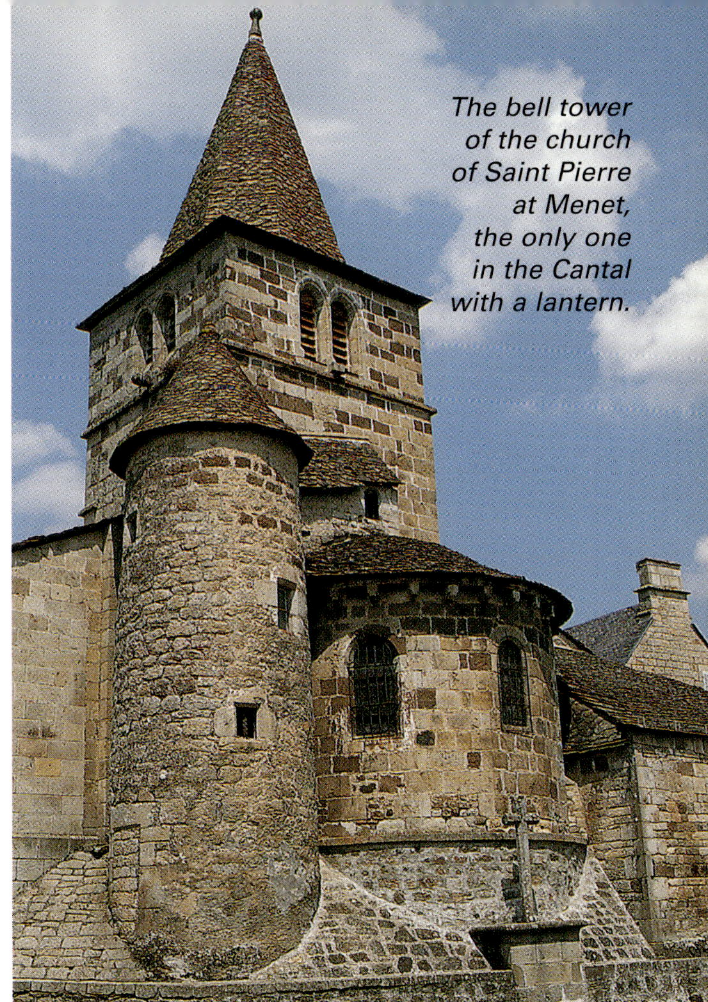

The bell tower of the church of Saint Pierre at Menet, the only one in the Cantal with a lantern.

Right - *A detail of the chevet of the church of Riom-ès-Mountains, whose decoration is similar to that of the Basse Auvergne, with its modillions and row of billets.*

Below, left - *The nave of the church of Saint Georges at Riom-ès-Mountains, with its pointed transverse arches.*
Right - *The capital of the Horsemen.*

The church of Trizac with its single apse.

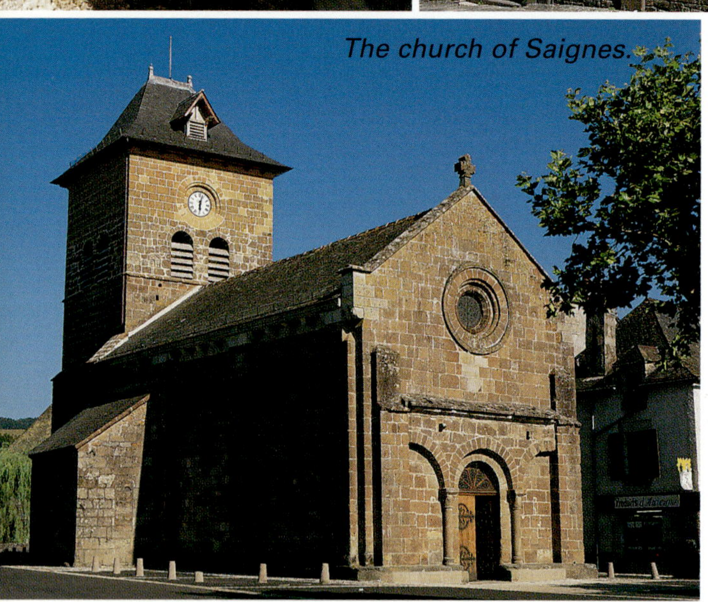

The church of Saignes.

The Burons of the Christ

"L'art roman est lui aussi une source. Complexe, lente à naître, chez nous dès ce magnifié XIe siècle où chaque val a connu sa chapelle. On a la richesse d'un choix unique, le privilège des pierres charpentées pour toujours, des vierges noires, des retenues d'eau lustrale, ces fonts baptismaux d'une paysannerie chrétienne (...). Il y a mille leçons à retrouver depuis Orcival, Saint Myon ou Châtel-de-Neuvre. Vingt autres à perdre. Ce morcellement des lieux de foi correspondait alors à celui des sols, des pâtures, des labours. Le paysage connaissait la dépense entière de chaque moment d'une vie, de la naissance à la fin. Ce sont ces burons du Christ, né sur la paille dix siècles plus tôt, qui rapprochèrent les gens."

Patrick Cloux, Auvergne immense et libre

Salguebrou!

The porch of the church at Ydes ends in a simple portal, the decoration of which consists of dragons playing under the engaged piers of the door and, above all, of a strange human figure sculpted in the round and which stands out from the tympanum. This face, which appears to be screaming, was considered locally to be a demon, known as "Salguebri" or "Salguebrou", that is "Sauve-toi... brr !" (Run for your life ... brr). The experts consider that it could represent a passage from the Apocalypse which says: "And then the inhabitants of the land heard a powerful voice from the sky".

The chevet of the church of Sainte-Croix at Saignes which is decorated by attractive sculptures. Top, left - *The "Lovers" modillion.*

The enthusiasm of the image makers

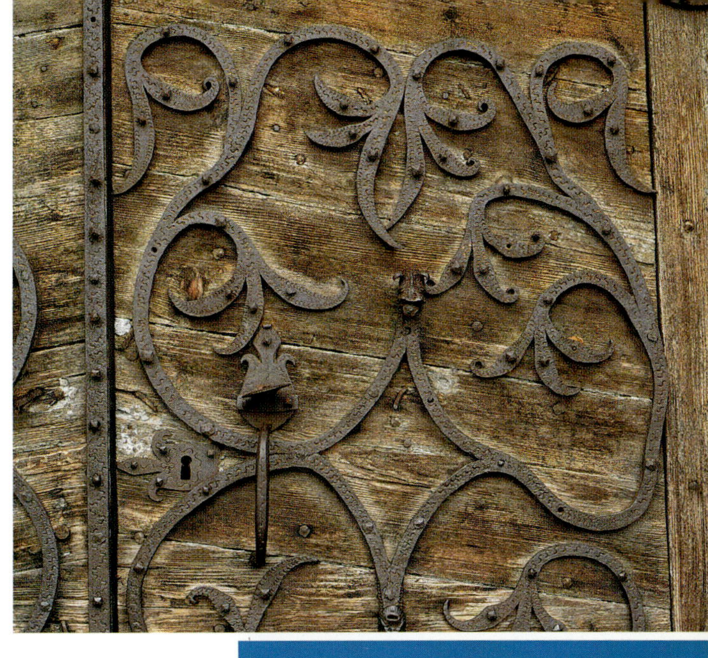

As at Mauriac for Notre-Dame-des-Miracles, the sculptors of the Middle Ages displayed their imagination in almost every church between Sumène and Maronne and the meaning of certain scenes remains unclear. At Saignes, the repertoire of the bases of columns, capitals and modillions goes from a lion pawing the ground to two tender lovers. The church at Ydes has a carved porch similar to that at Beaulieu-sur-Dordogne: it frames bas-reliefs representing the Annunciation and Daniel in the Lion's den.

Top, right - *The cast iron hinges of the church at Lanobre.*
Below - *The church of Saint Georges at Ydes has an apse remarkable for the drafting of its golden stone.*
Right - *The apse of the church at Ydes.*

Below, left - *The Annunciation in the porch at Ydes.*
Centre - *The chevet with its modillions and the Samson capital.*
Right - *The Romanesque pyx from the collection of relics and ornaments at Ydes and which was used as a box for communion wafers.*

Aerial view of Salers.

Mauriac, under the protection of Notre-Dame-des-Miracles

The ancient city of Mauriac became important after the foundation of a monastery that legend attributes to the daughter of Clovis. This institution dedicated to Saint Pierre and which depended on Sens, invoked the wrath of the bishop of Clermont, who had a second convent and the church of Notre-Dame built beside it. Between the two communities, the Lords of the manor and the inhabitants, conflicts were so frequent that the Pope himself had to intervene. Mauriac has lost the monastery of Saint Pierre, the excavation of which revealed the chapel of Saint Benoît and a superb 11th century chapter house. The basilica of Notre-Dame-des-Miracles, although extensively restored on several occasions, remains one of the most beautiful Romanesque buildings of the Haute Auvergne. In particular, the basilica has a magnificent portal, with the only tympanum in the Cantal, the theme of which is the Ascension, a magnificent example of the Languedoc school.

The recessed porch of the church of Salers. A capital on the door of Saint Martin-Cantalès.

Above, right - *Notre-Dame-des-Miracles, at Mauriac, the largest Romanesque shrine in the Haute Auvergne.*
Left - *The West portal, between two rustic 17th century towers.*

Right - *The West portal, with a Christ very similar to that of the north portal of Cahors Cathedral.*

Below, left - *The church of Anglards-de-Salers, without a transept, which is rare in Auvergne.*
Right - *The Romanesque font at Mauriac, with polychrome sculptures, one of the only ones remaining in the Auvergne.*

Above - *The discoid cross of Tourniac, of the 13th century, inspired by the Romanesque tradition.*
Below - *The choir of Saint Martin at Jaleyrac and the fresco of Christ in glory.*
Right - *Detail of the Gothic porch of Pleaux, the sculptures of which have remained Romanesque.*

The Romanesque crosses of the Cantal

Roads, crossings, bridges, mountain passes, peaks, fountains, squares and cemeteries; the horizons of the Auvergne are dotted with monumental crosses but, because they are so fragile very few of them are Romanesque. It is in the Haute Auvergne that these open air Romanesque crosses are the most common. Three have been dated with certainty. At Montsalvy, towards Boutelongue, stands the cross of Saint-Anne, a granite discoid cross raised in the 11th century on a rounded pedestal which marked the limit of the monastery founded by Saint Gausbert. At Pleaux, the solid Cross of the Crusade is a crossing monument, the Maltese cross of which is a reminder of the presence of the Knights Templar in the region during the 12th century. The Chaussenac cross at Cussac-Xaintrie, near the abbey of Brageac, is of the same period and also stands at a crossing: it consists of a notched discoid cross, on which Christ, with his legs crossed, is nailed, in the Languedoc manner.

Above - *The church of Brageac and its wild setting.*
Left - *The 13th century reliquary cross from the collection of relics and ornaments at Brageac.*

Hidden Treasures

The recent restoration of the shrine at Jaleyrac revealed another facet of the talent of the artists of the Romanesque period, whose frescoes are among the most interesting in the Cantal. Close by, the modest church of Moussages houses the Madonna of Claviers, which is considered to be the most remarkable in the Haute Auvergne. Legend has it that the Lord of Scorailles donated this statue on the eve of his departure for the crusade, in 1098. Nevertheless, the work would appear to date from the 12th century. On the other hand, it is true that on their return from the Holy Land, Gui and Raoul de Scorailles were responsible for the foundation of the Benedictine nunnery at Brageac. Its church, magnificently located overlooking the gorge of the Auze, is a model of architectural purity and stone drafting.

The Madonna of Moussages.

The Black Madonna of the Maronne

In days gone by, the village of Saint Christophe, perched above the gorge of the Maronne, had two castles. Now, all that remains is the private Romanesque chapel, which conceals its wall belfry and stone roof in the middle of an enclosure in a rocky hollow and which houses one of the beautiful Black Madonnas of the Cantal. Although the Infant Jesus she is carrying in her left arm is somewhat exotic in appearance, with his Asiatic eyes, this effigy is very probably that of a truly Auvergnat Romanesque Madonna. For generations, pilgrims came to worship her after climbing the stairs leading to the chapel of Notre-Dame-du-Château on their knees.

The church of Girgols, typical of the West Cantal.

The church of Tournemire, which still has a Romanesque porch.

Thick, black stone walls

"L'Auvergne est hivernale, venteuse et montagnarde. Pour lutter contre les ténèbres, la pluie, les terreurs du solstice, l'Auvergnat se groupe comme les moutons afin de mieux résister au vent. Puis il bâtit autour de lui des murs de pierre épais et noirs, qui ont donné des châteaux célèbres, comme Tournoël, des églises fortes comme Royat, de grands gibets comme à Allègre et le style roman auvergnat."

Alexandre Vialatte,
Dernières nouvelles de l'Homme. *Juillard*

Above - *The church of Jou-sous-Montjou, whose wall belfry rises above the triumphal arch inside.*
Below - *The church of Lascelles, characteristic of the Jordanne valley.*

The church of Saint-Pierre at Vic-sur-Cèr

In memory of Saint Géraud

Aurillac owes its development to the "Good Count" Géraud, who founded an abbey which depended directly on Rome in about 900, on the banks of the Jordanne, at the foot of his château. Rich, impressive and influential, this institution was proud to give Cluny its second abbot, Odon and the first French Pope in Christendom, Gerbert, a former shepherd from the Planèze. Aurillac, which became the second city in the diocese, was given a large Romanesque church, which Pope Urban II consecrated in 1095. A few stone fragments from this church are conserved in the chapel to Saint Géraud.

Certain nearby shrines reflect the golden age of the abbey of Saint Géraud, in particular the church of Lascelle, which was one of its priories, like those at Girgols and Laroquevieille, in the same part of the Cantalès.

Below - *The 17th century statue of Saint Géraud, who is holding a model of his abbey.*
Right - *The serpentine fountain saved from the cloister of Saint Géraud*
Bottom, right - *Samson, one of the pre-romanesque capitals of the abbey church.*

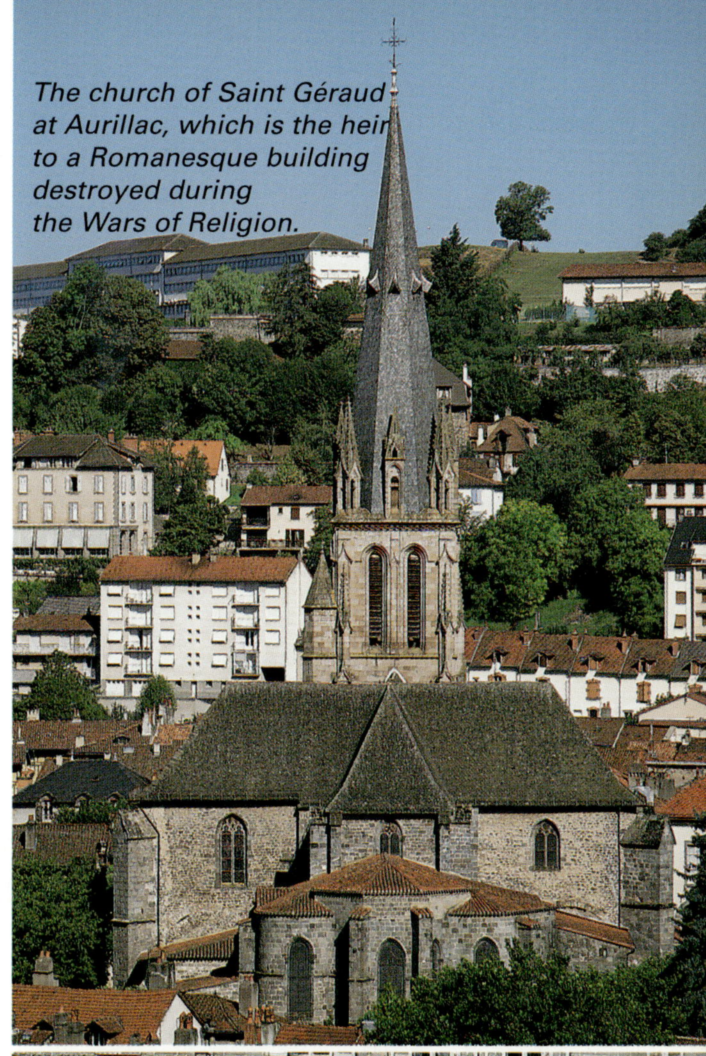

The church of Saint Géraud at Aurillac, which is the heir to a Romanesque building destroyed during the Wars of Religion.

Above, top - *The arcaded chevet of the church at Saint Urcize.*
Bottom - *The collegiate church of Montsalvy and the priory buildings.*

PILGRIMAGE SITES

On the southern fringes of the Haute Auvergne, several sites used to be marked by the passage of pilgrims to Compostela who came to pray over the tomb of Saint Géraud, before the relics of Saint Césaire at Maurs or those of Saint Georges and Sainte Foy at Conques. Therefore, the church of Saint Urcize, the only one in the Cantal that has an ambulatory, is a mixture of styles of the traditions of the Rouergue and the Auvergne, like that at Montsalvy, the only Romanesque church of the Châtaigneraie. The church of Saint-Pierre at Maurs houses the bust reliquary of Saint Césaire, the bishop of Arles, an effigy whose evocative power is as strong as that of the statue of Sainte Foy at Conques.

DE LA ROCHE ET D'UN RÊVE...

"L'église de Saint Urcize, un peu basse, est une des plus belles romanes du Cantal. Son abside à chapelles rayonnantes, ses lucarnes, ses mosaïques diaprées, feraient penser qu'elle s'est bâtie comme de soi, de la roche et d'un rêve ; simplement elle a imité ces natures que sont le nid de bourdons, la coque d'escargot, les touffes de fleurs dans les amas de pierres rondes. Et certaines vieilles maisons, dans ces rues resserrées, semblent pareillement s'être faites de soi-même. Quelque follet de la montagne aura endormi le maçon, le charpentier ; et c'est son songe à lui, qui a pris corps."

Henri Pourrat, En Auvergne. *Arthaud*

Below, left - *The crook of Saint Césaire at Maurs.*
Centre - *The discoid cross of Montsalvy.*
Right - *The Crucifix of Montsalvy.*

The bust reliquary of Saint Césaire, of silver and gilded copper, with cabochons of emeralds, saphires, topazes, ivory and coloured glass.

«L'éclat sombre des prunelles, la démesure du nez, du menton, l'énormité des mains, l'une bénissante, l'autre accueillante, faites pour être vues de loin, au cours des processions, portées sur des échines humaines, ont ici, dans leur rutilante immobilité, quelque chose d'hallucinant et de formidable.»

Jean Anglade,
Auvergne. *Nathan*

The chapel of Saint Ilpize, overlooking one of the most beautiful sites in the Allier gorge.
Inset, left - *The pilgrimage to Compostela, today.*
Right - *The 15th century statue of Saint Jacques which stands in a niche in the basilica of Saint Julien at Brioude.*

The pilgrims' landmarks

The worshippers who continue to follow in the footsteps of pilgrims from the past, still find a large number of landmarks to guide them to Compostela, particularly on the via podensis (from Le Puy), one of the most popular routes. At Le Puy, the pilgrim first sees an oratory dedicated to their patron Saint, in the rue Saint Jacques, followed by the "pilgrims' cross" at Le Chier, then that of Monistrol-d'Allier which shows the pilgrim in his traditional clothes; via the chapel of Saint-Jacques at Saint Privat-d'Allier, pilgrims reach Saugues, where they never fail to pray for the protection of the Virgin Mary. Pilgrims feared wolves, brigands and blizzards when crossing the Aubrac. The village of the same name still has its "blizzard bell" which was rung when it was foggy. As they cross the rivers on their route, the rest of the road through the Aveyron is easier and again our pilgrims have a succession of landmarks to guide them, from the stone cross on the bridge over the Boralde at Saint Chély, on which a pilgrim is carved, to the flamboyant statue of Saint Jacques in the porch of the church at Estaing.

FROM BRIOUDE TO THE ROADS TO SANTIAGO DE COMPOSTELA

Brioude, an immense stone reliquary

Around the tomb of Saint Julien

Over the centuries, Saint Julien of Brioude was revered almost to the same extent as Saint Martin of Tours and it follows that the basilica at Brioude is the most important Romanesque church in the Auvergne. The town entered history in 304, after Julien, a Roman soldier converted to Christianity, had fled Vienne to take refuge in the Auvergne, where he was found and beheaded. His head which was returned to Vienne, was buried beside the body of his companion Ferréol, whilst two old men, Arcons and Ilpize, buried the body of the martyr at Brioude, following which their youth was miraculously restored.

Brioude then became a place of pilgrimage, helped by the fact that it was on the road to Le Puy, Saint Gilles and Compostela. The 11th and 12th centuries were the golden age of pilgrimages, but before the impressive period of the canon-counts of Saint Julien who built the present church, several monuments had preceded it, like a series of reliquaries around the tomb of the Saint, whose crypt survives. The basilica uses all the possible hues of Auvergne stone, red sandstone, limestone, blackish brown or dark red basalt, granulite, grey and pink marbles, to which are added the polychromy of the bell tower roof and the typically Auvergnat mosaic of the wide apse. Outside, one may appreciate the harmonious perspective of the chevet with five apses, the last great Romanesque church in the Auvergne.

The south door which has retained its Romanesque iron work and bronze knockers.

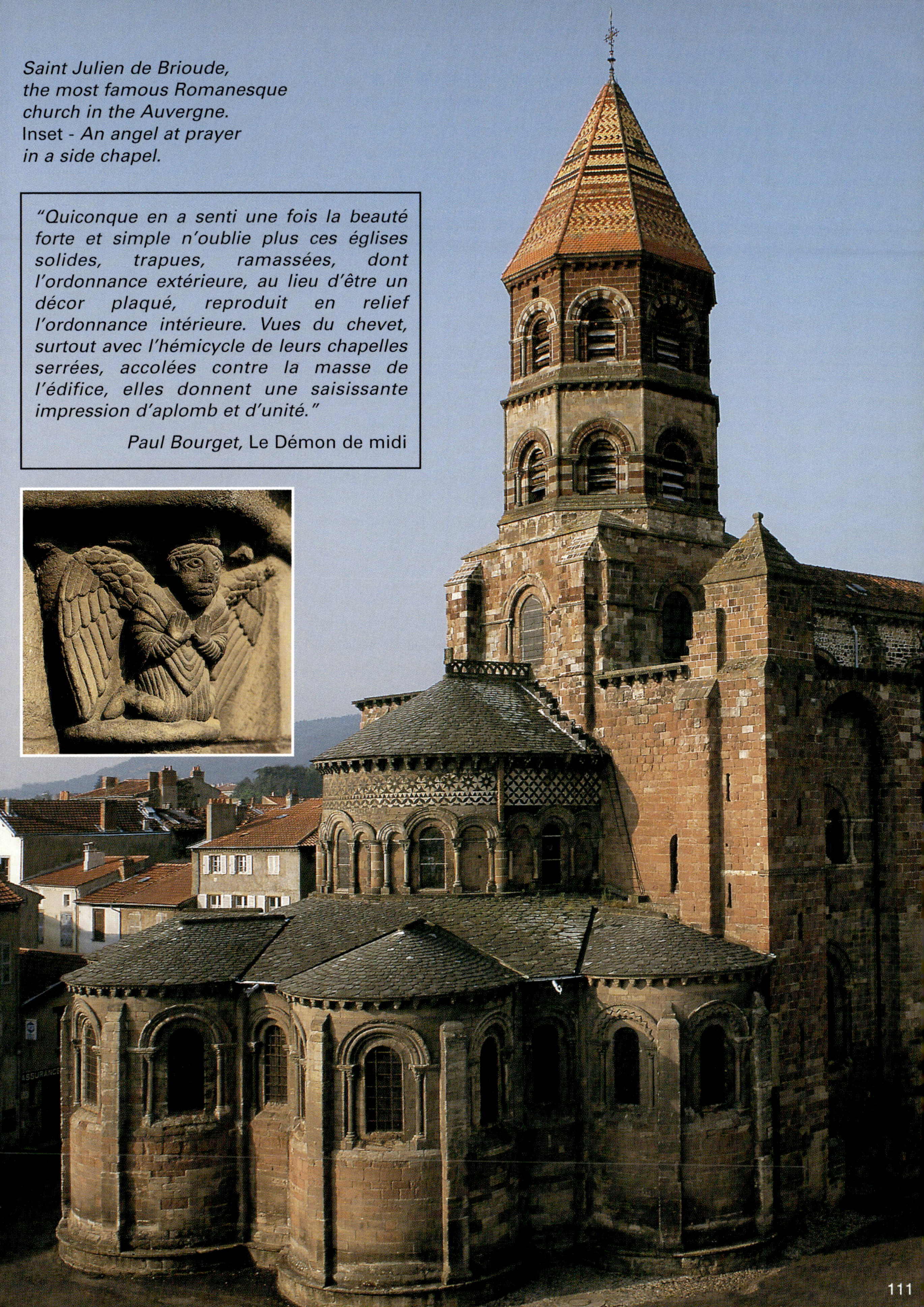

Saint Julien de Brioude, the most famous Romanesque church in the Auvergne.
Inset - *An angel at prayer in a side chapel.*

> *"Quiconque en a senti une fois la beauté forte et simple n'oublie plus ces églises solides, trapues, ramassées, dont l'ordonnance extérieure, au lieu d'être un décor plaqué, reproduit en relief l'ordonnance intérieure. Vues du chevet, surtout avec l'hémicycle de leurs chapelles serrées, accolées contre la masse de l'édifice, elles donnent une saisissante impression d'aplomb et d'unité."*
>
> *Paul Bourget,* Le Démon de midi

Paved with pebbles from the Allier, the wide nave of the church of Saint Julien de Brioude is decorated with capitals of great variety, which betrays the length of its construction, undertaken by three or four generations of master builders.

The force of the Auvergne

"Un pays entre les pays. Pays d'extrêmes, fait de sourcilleux rochers et de plaines unies, le plus plantureux de tous, et, de tous ceux qui ne sont pas aux frontières, le plus sauvage (...). C'est parce qu'elle est pétrie de contraires, l'Auvergne, qu'elle est vraiment une grande chose de nature. Le style roman, la bourrée, le jansénisme ne font que manifester diversement la même vigueur, tantôt repliée, tantôt tournée à la fougue."

Henri Pourrat,
Ceux d'Auvergne. *Albin Michel*

REFINED DECORATION

We enter the basilica through a magnificent two storied narthex, which is the oldest and most interesting part of the building, in architectural terms. Then the decoration attracts our attention, starting with the famous capitals. They include asses playing the lyre, mermaids and the Minotaur. Recent work has restored the ancient paving of the nave of multi-coloured pebbles from the Allier and priceless Romanesque frescos, in particular the four horsemen of the Apocalypse, the saints on the vaults of both apsidioles and the Last Judgement in the narthex.

Above - *The 13th century fresco on the ceiling of the chapel of Saint-Michel, on the first floor of the narthex of Saint Julien de Brioude: Christ in Glory giving his blessing, the punishment of the Fallen Angels and the Triumph of Virtue over Vice.*
Right - *One of the king's head brackets in the choir.*

Famous Benedictine Monasteries

In Lavaudieu and Blesle, the Brivadois has two of the most interesting monuments of the Romanesque period. Complementing an already picturesque village, the monastery of Lavaudieu is the only one in the Auvergne not to have suffered during the Revolution and its cloister is unique in the province. Between the refectory and a simple abbey church, the wooden gallery and irregular columns of this small cloister are quite charming. The monastery was spared thanks to its modest size, but this only goes to heighten the impression of serenity of the "Vallée de Dieu".

Left - *The fresco in the refectory at Lavaudieu, with a huge Christ in glory surrounded by the symbols of the Evangelists.*
Below - *A detail showing the Apostles, on either side of the Virgin Mary at the bottom of the fresco.*

The Ganivelle at Auzon

Perched at the top of the village, on a pedestal of rock, the church of Auzon, which houses one of the most beautiful Romanesque Crucifixes in the province, is reached via two ramps which run along its southern flank and end in staircases. As at Brioude, where they meet, there stands a "ganivelle", a majestic porch. It features figured capitals showing the Nativity of Christ. Behind this shelter, the door of the church has retained its Romanesque leaves, with fine ironwork and nails, all of which have different heads.

Fiancés at the Abbey

The Benedictine nunnery at Lavaudieu was founded by Saint Robert in 1058, soon after he had founded the abbey of La Chaise-Dieu. Legend has it that he did so to avoid rekindling the love between Simon de Crépy, the count of Bar-sur-Aube, who asked to be admitted to La Chaise-Dieu, and his fiancée Judith, the daughter of Robert the Count of Auvergne, who occupied the nuns' building, near the main abbey. These two characters really existed and devoted their lives to God, but the dates contradict the legend, since Judith only took her vows at Lavaudieu in 1077.

Blesle, the Ladies' church

Hidden on the edge of the gorge of the Allagnon, the jewel in the crown of Blesle is its ancient Romanesque abbey church in its venerable urban setting. The complex architectural history of the abbey church of Saint-Pierre extends from the Carolingian period to the end of the Romanesque age. The same is true of its decoration, from a marble altar donated to the founder by the Pope in 865, to the nailed, 12th century doors and including a large, polychrome Madonna. The nave is raised and this "chœur des Dames" was, in days gone by, intended to separate nuns of noble origins from ordinary parishioners during services.

Left - *Notre-Dame du Cheylat, the 13th century Madonna in Glory from the collection of relics and ornaments at Blesle.*
Below - *The choir of the church of Saint-Pierre at Blesle.*

The Romanesque porch with its arch mouldings of the southern transept.
Right - *The polychrome wooden crucifix from the collection of relics and ornaments at Blesle.*

A curious decor for the canonesses

In about 870, Ermengarde, the wife of the Count of Auvergne Bernard II, founded a nunnery at Blesle dedicated to Saint Pierre. Until the Revolution, successive generations of canonesses had before them quite surprising Romanesque sculptures. The capitals of the choir windows alternate biblical scenes with a fantastic bestiary of birds with crossed beaks, lions in confrontation, winged griffins and mermaids with two tails. Even more astonishing, the capitals outside are carved with winged dragons with their necks intertwined and tails knotted, two horsemen face to face, one of whom is strangely androgynous and, above all a woman with voluptuous breasts who is sensuously nursing a serpent and a salamander. On one side, the hind legs of the salamander are gripping the lip and thigh of a naked man, with a grimacing face and who is wearing a crown, whilst on the other, a second naked man who is carrying a bag. The serpent emerges from the mouth of a second naked man. This is probably a variation on the usual themes of lust and avarice.

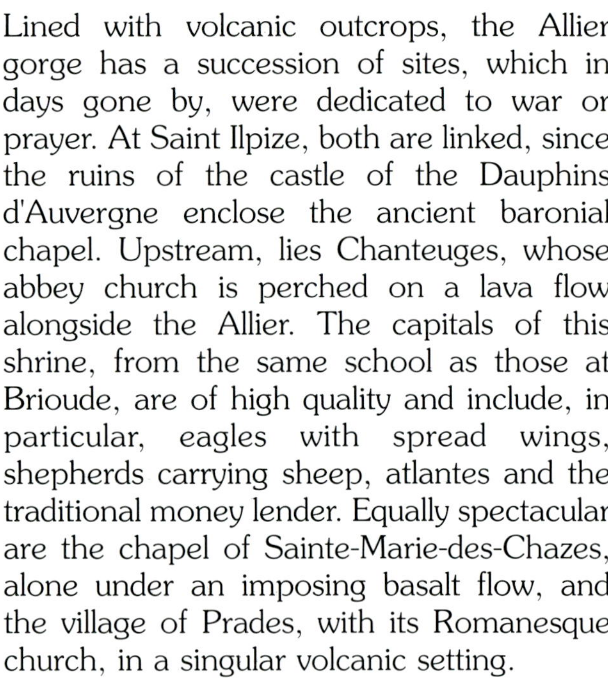

MOVING DOWN THE GORGES

Lined with volcanic outcrops, the Allier gorge has a succession of sites, which in days gone by, were dedicated to war or prayer. At Saint Ilpize, both are linked, since the ruins of the castle of the Dauphins d'Auvergne enclose the ancient baronial chapel. Upstream, lies Chanteuges, whose abbey church is perched on a lava flow alongside the Allier. The capitals of this shrine, from the same school as those at Brioude, are of high quality and include, in particular, eagles with spread wings, shepherds carrying sheep, atlantes and the traditional money lender. Equally spectacular are the chapel of Sainte-Marie-des-Chazes, alone under an imposing basalt flow, and the village of Prades, with its Romanesque church, in a singular volcanic setting.

Top, left - *Prades, in the Allier gorge.*
Right - *The chapel of Saint Ilpize.*
Opposite - *The Byzantine style Crucifix of Lavoûte-Chilhac, which came from the leper hospital of Sainte-Madeleine de Chilhac.*
Below - *The chapel of Sainte-Marie-des-Chazes, a pilgrimage site lost in the Allier gorge.*

Chanteuges overlooking the Allier gorge, with Saint Arcons in the distance.
Below, left - *The abbey church of Chanteuges, the low profile of which is due to a 15th century restoration.* Right - *The village of Chanteuges.*
Bottom - *Three capitals from Chanteuges,*
the calm after the storm... the Good Shepherd and... eagles with spread wings.

SAINT-RÉMY AND POLIGNAC

Isolated between Loudes and Bains, the church of Saint Rémy combines a massive silhouette, a bell wall and a highly recessed door-way, typical of the mountain churches of the Cantal. In the shadow of a site and castle which attract all the attention, the church of Saint Martin in the little town of Polignac was built in the 11th and 12th centuries before being decorated with a wide Gothic door-way. Under its arches, stands the primitive square choir with capitals showing, in particular, old people adoring the Lamb of God and men pointing at animals and, in the apse, frescos of the Last Judgement and Saint Michel.

Above, left - *A detail of one of the very rustic capitals of Saint Rémy.*
Right - *The church of Saint Rémy, with its bell wall and deep porch.*
Below - *The church of Saint Martin at Polignac.*

The "Ox Killing Stone" of Saint Paulien

The former Gallo-Roman capital of the Velay, Saint Paulien has a mysterious "ox killing stone" which is now the base for a cross, in front of the collegiate church of Saint Georges. The sanctuary includes ancient stone fragments, whilst certain capitals of the absidioles are sculpted with interlaced patterns inspired by Celtic art. Of the seven absidial chapels, four are Romanesque. The collegiate church has a huge apse with an ambulatory, combined with a single nave. The absence of internal walls, which led to the use of powerful buttresses, reminds us of the Romanesque churches of the Languedoc.

Above - *An aerial view of the church of Saint Paulien.*
Right - *A detail of the chevet, with an absidiole and a flying buttress.*

The former garndeur of Chamalières-sur-Loire

Chamalières-sur-Loire was one of the spiritual centres of the Velay, since it was home to a priory that depended on Le Monastier, whose fame lay in the possession of the relics of Saint Clou, donated by Charlemagne, and those of Saint Gilles d'Arles. The river swept away the monastery buildings, with the exception of a few arcades of the cloisters and the present church of Saint Gilles is the main reminder of its importance. It was built in the 12th century and has changed little. The plainness of its external appearance highlights the illustrated and painted door leaves, the unfortunately severely damaged illuminations now protected against the weather. Inside, the visitor may admire an immense semi-circular apse which originally had an ambulatory and the famous Romanesque "prophets' font", bas-reliefs and frescos.

Above - *A detail of the old door leaves of the church at Chamalières-sur-Loire and the building as a whole.*
Bottom - *The vast oven-shaped apse of the church at Chamalières-sur-Loire.*

The Influence of Le Monastier

Le Monastier-sur-Gazeille was founded in 680 by Calminius, count of the Auvergne and the abbey church of the town is heir to this first monastic foundation in the Velay. The monastery, which was destroyed by the Saracens, was built around the church and the castle abbey that may still be seen today, and was for many years as influential as the monastery of La Chaise-Dieu. The abbey church houses particularly magnificent treasures, the main item of which is a Romanesque reliquary bust of Saint Chaffre, or Saint Théofrède, who was the second abbot of Le Monastier. They also include two rare 10th century Byzantine silks.

Top, left - *The façade of the abbey church at Le Monastier.*
Right - *The silver plated wooden reliquary bust of Saint Théofrède.*
Bottom - *A detail from one of the Byzantine silks which form part of Le Monastier's treasures.*

Le Puy-en-Velay, the gateway to Compostela

In days gone by, Le Puy-en-Velay was one of the gathering points in France for pilgrims on their way to Santiago de Compostela, along with Paris, Vézelay and Arles. This important position is confirmed by the fact that the first pilgrim to which history refers was Godescalk, bishop of Le Puy, who took the road to Galicia in 950.

This opening to the Iberian peninsula can still be seen in the town today; the chapel of Saint-Michel-d'Aiguilhe and the Cathedral of Notre-Dame, its main Romanesque monuments, show extensive signs of Mozarabic influences. Eastern influences are also due to the return from the Crusades, since it was the bishop of Le Puy, Adhémar de Monteil, that Pope Urban II named to lead the first Crusade in 1095. Nevertheless, these buildings retain an architecture based on that of the Limousin and their decorations reveal Gallo-Roman inspiration in common with the Auvergne.

Le Puy was the scene of one of the oldest visions of the Virgin Mary, in about 420. Since then, popular devotion has continued uninterrupted, taking over from beliefs from the mists of time, since the flat stone of a dolmen, known as the "pierre des fièvres" (fever stone) stands at the top of one of the grand stairways.

The main object of devotion was a Black Madonna, destroyed during the Revolution, a faithful reproduction of which shows that it was true to the ancient Auvergnat tradition, except that the Infant Jesus is not shown giving his blessing, and that his hands, like those of the Virgin Mary, are curiously white.

SAINT MICHEL D'AIGUILHE, THE EIGHTH WONDER OF THE WORLD

The volcanic needle which rises at the gates of Le Puy was transfigured more than a thousand years ago by the construction of a shrine, the fine silhouette of which extends its peak. Dedicated to Saint Michel, the building is reached by a stairway of 268 steps overlooked by a Romanesque portal with an Auvergnat lintel. At the end of this difficult climb lies "une espèce de petit bijou d'architecture" (a little architectural gem) to quote Mérimée. A moving vision indeed of the polychrome front of the church of Saint-Michel d'Aiguilhe, with its trefoil portal with Byzantine style sculptures. The "Orient" also inspired the frescos and architecture of the chapel, capped by a pyramidal bell tower comparable to that of the cathedral.

Opposite - *The Rocher d'Aiguilhe, overlooking the Borne. A Byzantine Madonna on a reliquary cross. The trefoil portal of Saint-Michel d'Aiguilhe.*
Below - *The irregular layout of the chapel of Saint-Michel d'Aiguilhe shows how the masons adapted to the shape of the volcanic needle.*
Inset - *The Spanish looking Romanesque Crucifix from the collection of relics and ornaments of the chapel was probably brought back from Compostela by a pilgrim.*

A cathedral with a navel and ears...

Like Saint-Michel d'Aiguilhe, the Cathedral of Notre-Dame of Le Puy is in perfect harmony with its setting, which it overlooks from an unusual bell tower inspired by the Pharos of Alexandria. The main front, which rises magnificently over the steps leading up to it, combines false wall belfries and sophisticated stone mosaic decoration. Behind this lofty front, the nave is capped with cupolas buttressed by the aisles, an archaic Eastern form, which matches the plan of the building. For a long time, access to the cathedral was through the Papal door, which covers one of the oldest Auvergnat saddle back lintels dating back to the 6th century. Originally, the pilgrims entered the shrine "through its navel and left through the ears", according to a 17th century expression; that is through a tunnel leading directly to the front of the choir, an arrangement that recent work has restored. Whilst the architecture of Notre-Dame du Puy was not widely imitated in the Auvergne, its painted and carved decorations have, on the other hand, been models for the entire province. This is also true in so far as the organisation of these figures is concerned, like a Bible in images intended for the edification of the illiterate masses. Since, long before the kings and princes, it was the people who made Le Puy what it was, the Lourdes of the Middle Ages.

Above left - *In the west hand gallery, the portrait of Saint Michel, which at 5.55 metres high is the largest of its type in France.*
Centre - *An overall view of the Cathedral and the monastic buildings, with the original Arabic chimney of the cloister.*
Right - *Reproduced by Philippe Kæppelin after a drawing by Faujas de Saint Fond, the Black Madonna of Le Puy, the original of which dated back to the 10th century.*

The Old Town of Le Puy, at the foot of the Cathedral and the statue of Notre-Dame de France.

The martyrdom of Saint Catherine of Alexandria, in one of the side chapels of the left hand gallery.

The baptistery of Saint Jean, the oldest religious monument in Le Puy, opens through a Romanesque door-way preceded by two stone lions in the Lombardy style. Its single nave ends in a triumphal arch leading to a semi-circular apse topped with arcatures. The opposite end of the nave is laid out as a gallery. The baptistery, which is built on Carlolingian walls, includes Gallo-roman stone sculpted with friezes or Cupids. It is linked to the cathedral by the arch of the porch of Saint Jean and to the building of the Clergeons by a vaulted arch under which begins the rue du Cloître, an assembly which illustrates the original "cathedral group", of which it is the sole remnant.

The apse of the baptistery of Saint Jean, with the sculptures of the Pilgrims to Santiago de Compostela by Dominique Kæppelin.

Frescos of the cathedral
Below - *The fresco of the Madonna and Child on the west side in the porch of the great staircase.*
Opposite - *Saint Etienne, a detail of the fresco of the Transfiguration, in the western porch of the great staircase.*

"The Finest Cloister in European Christendom"

Emile Mâle, the eminent specialist in mediaeval religious art, says we should take the time to visit the cathedral cloisters. As if to echo the Arabic figures who sing praise to the glory of Allah on the cathedral's cedar doors, the cloisters remind us of the mosque at Cordoba, with its white, black and red voussoirs and Arab inspired stone marquetry work. Apart from these surprising similarities, the sculptures in the cloister are eminently Christian and describe the struggle the faithful have to make to reach salvation; for example, the capital showing a female centaur fleeing from a centaur to escape his lust, whilst the bliss of those who enter Heaven is shown by two doves drinking from a vase. Similarly, the frieze which runs under the roof, has evocative scenes representing the three main temptations, lust, gluttony and vainglory.

The chapter house, or chapel of the dead, where canons were buried from the 17th century, and its late 12th century fresco of the Crucifixion which was completed in less than a hundred days.

The capital of the struggle between Good and Evil. The capital of the female centaur, in the West gallery. The gate to the cloister, which is one of the finest examples of Romanesque ornamental ironwork; its precious appearance is due to the punch and chisel marks with which its surface is covered.

Above - *The chapel of Notre-Dame d'Estours.*
Left - *The Madonna of Estours who inspired an important pilgrimage. She appeared to two shepherd boys and asked them to build a chapel.*

Below, left - *The church of Saint Médard at Saugues and its Auvergnat bell-tower.*
Right - *The inscrutable face of the Madonna of Saugues.*

Under the sign of Saint Roch

When they left Le Puy, pilgrims had one of the most difficult parts of the road to Santiago before them, with the crossing of the Allier gorge and the Aubrac highlands. This thousand year old road is remarkably preserved as far as Saugues and it is clear that the cult of Saint Roch was very strong. There are still many chapels dedicated to this protector of pilgrims, but the one most dear to their hearts is the one dedicated to Notre-Dame of Estours. Built on a wild site in the gorge of the Seuge and housing a 12th century polychrome Madonna, it is still the focus of a fervent cult. Close by, Monistrol-d'Allier lies in a magnificent gorge, set off by the Romanesque church of Saint Pierre. Saugues, the former capital of the Gévaudan, was an important staging post and gathering point for pilgrims from the Auvergne, who found the comfort of a monastery-hospital within its walls. The town is visible from a distance thanks to the collegiate church of Saint Médard, originally built on the model of the Romanesque basilicas of the Auvergne. For at least eight centuries, the faithful have prayed to a Madonna in Glory carrying the Infant Jesus giving his blessing, a sculpture brought alive by gentle polychromy. It is worth noting that the collection of relics and ornaments of the collegiate church includes a rare Romanesque chasuble embroidered by the Ladies of the Court of Charles X.

Above - *Alone in the vastness of the Aubrac, the Rodde cross is one of the crosses that show pilgrims the way between Le Puy and Conques.*
Right - *The bells of Chanaleilles rang continuously when it was foggy.*
Below, left - *A ford near Nasbinals.*
Inset - *The church of Nasbinals which depended on the Dômerie of Aubrac.*
Right - *Notre-Dame-des-Pauvres, the 11th century Dômerie of Aubrac, a reminder of the times when the orders of chivalry protected pilgrims.*

Sainte Foy de Conques, the model for pilgrimage churches

The presence of precious relics, including those of Sainte Foy the famous virgin – stolen from Agen by a monk from the Rouergue! - made Conques one of the most important pilgrimage sites in France. In 1040, this monastery, first sponsored by Charlemagne, started the construction of a special monumental basilica to house, both its clergy and the throngs desperate for miracles. Sainte-Foy of Conques thus became the model for the great Romanesque pilgrimage churches, before Saint Cernin in Toulouse, before Saint Martial of Limoges, before Saint Martin of Tours and even before Santiago de Compostela. This Auvergnat Romanesque form of art characteristic of the Rouergue also inspired humbler shrines, such as the church at Perse, dedicated to Saint Hilarian, which was for many years the parish church of Espalion.

On the site of the martyrdom of Saint Hilarian, the church of Perse d'Espalion and its carved portal.
Inset - *A Romanesque Madonna in a niche outside and which is inspired by Auvergnat Madonnas in Glory.*
Right - *Under a wall belfry, the chevet of the church of Perse, with its pentagonal apse decorated with engaged columns, as at Conques.*

Below, left - *The Romanesque chapel of Saint-Pierre de la Bouysse, at Saint Côme-d'Olt.*
Right - *Estaing, on the Lot, which in the 12th century only had a wooden bridge.*

"Autrefois asile des bêtes fauves et des oiseaux mélodieux, ce lieu était resté inconnu de l'homme que rebutait son aspect sauvage." Ermold le Noir (IXe siècle).

ROMANESQUE ART AS PRAYER

To enter the abbey church of Sainte-Foy at Conques, is to change dimensions, so powerfully does the central nave spring up toward Heaven. This impression is achieved by an architecture reduced to its bare essentials, but which uses all the resources of the Mediaeval science of numbers, whose subtlety we rediscover. Before feeling this call to prayer throughout his being, the worshipper is invited to gaze upon the sumptuous tympanum of the Last Judgement over the western portal of the abbey church. Exceptional in its dimensions, the number of figures, the originality of the way in which they are carved, in a word, its beauty, this sculpted work is very clearly organised around a huge Christ, which catches the eye.

Top, right - *The cloister at Conques, with its serpentine basin.*
Top, left - *The Knights' capital, in the cloister.*
Bottom, left - *The peak of Romanesque sculpture, with Byzantine and Carolingian influences, the tympanum at Conques and its host of figures.*
Bottem, right - *Christ, presiding over the destiny of humanity.*

TRÉSOR MILLÉNAIRE

After achieving greatness through the cult of relics, the abbey at Conques quite naturally became a centre for gold and silver work. The treasure of Sainte Foy is witness to a thousand years of religious art. Gold, silver, ivory, jewels and precious stones, often of ancient origin, from the abundant donations made to the abbey, which were transformed in a monastic workshop which operated from the 9th to 16th centuries. The masterpiece of this collection of relics and ornaments is Sainte Foy in glory, a statue reliquary, the embossed golden head of which, dating back to the dawn of Christianity, is mounted on a body and throne created in about 966, when the relics arrived. Adorned over the centuries with multicoloured gems, this statue, with its strange expression, is the symbol of persisting faith on the roads to Compostela.

Top, left - *The letter A donated by Charlemagne (9th century), the first letter of the alphabet symbolising the preference the Emperor had for Conques.*
Top, right - *The reliquary of Pepin of the 9th, 10th and 11th centuries, is the oldest item in the treasury.*

Opposite, left - *Sainte Foy in Glory.*

Right - *The late 11th century portable alabaster altar, decorated with enamel work on gilded copper.*

Bottom, left - *The lantern of Bégon III, who was abbot of Conques from 1083 to 1107.*
Bottem, centre - *The 13th century "Saint Georges" arm reliquary; Saint Georges was a monk at Conques and bishop of Lodève.*
Bottom, right - *A reliquary decorated with Merovingian and Carolingian fragments.*

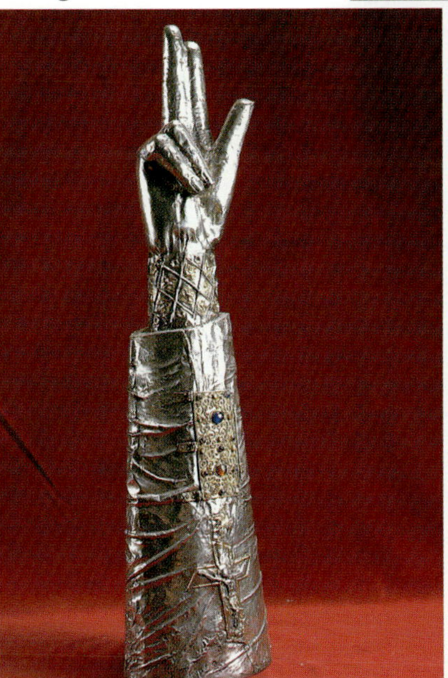

NIÈVRE
CHER
SAÔNE-ET-LOIRE
ALLIER
BOURBONNAIS
CREUSE
PUY-DE-DÔME
LOIRE
Allier
Sioule
Lurcy-Lévy
Franchesse
Cérilly
Agonges
Bourbon-L'Archambault
St-Menoux
Moulins
Neuvy
Yzeure
Ygrande
Autry-Issards
Souvigny
Coulandon
Cosne-d'Allier
Meillers
St-Désiré
Buxières-les-Mines
La Chapelaude
Le Montet
Châtel-de-Neuvre
Chappes
Huriel
Domérat
Montluçon
Jaligny
Neuilly-en-Donjon
Bert
Montmarault
Commentry
Bransat
Néris-les-Bains
St-Pourçain-sur-Sioule
St-Bonnet-de-Four
Bayet
Lapalisse
Langy
Droiturier
Chantelle
Barberier
Ste-Thérence
Bellenaves
Jenzat
St-Germain-des-Fossés
Veauce
Vicq
St-Pont
Seuillet
Escurolles
Châtel-Montagne
Ébreuil
Cognat
Vichy
Gannat
Biozat
Arronnes
0
20
40
60 km
PUY-DE-DÔME
LOIRE
Lyon
St-Étienne
Auzon
Lempdes
St-Hilaire
Léotoing
Azerat
Blesle
Bournoncle-St-Pierre
La Chaise-Dieu
Espalem
Brioude
HAUTE-LOIRE
Lavaudieu
Monistrol-sur-Loire
Loire
Allier
Domeyrat
Saint-Ilpize
Mazeyrat-Aurouze
St-Paulien
Chamalières
Lavoûte-Chilhac
Yssingeaux
Arlet
Peyrusse
Polignac
Via Podensis
Chaspuzac
Aiguilhe
VELAY
Chanteuges
Ste-Marie-des-Ch.
St-Rémy
Le Puy-en-Velay
Saint-Arcons-d'Allier
St-Julien-Chapteuil
Prades
Vals-près-le-Puy
Estours
St-Privat-d'Allier
Saugues
Monistrol-d'Allier
Le Monastier
Chanaleilles
Alleyras
Arlempdes
0
20
40
60 km
CANTAL
Saint-Chély-d'Apcher
Chemin de St-Jacques-de-Compostelle
St-Alban-sur-Limagnole
Truyère
AVEYRON
Aumont-Aubrac
Lot
Entraygues-sur-Truyère
Nasbinals
Saint-Chély-d'Aubrac
Aubrac
ARDÈCHE
Estaing
La Rode
LOZÈRE
Cahors
Conques
Espalion
Saint-Côme-d'Olt
Sainte-Eulalie-d'Olt
Église-de-Perse
ROUERGUE
Bozouls
Roquelaure
GÉVAUDAN
Clairvaux
Saint-Geniez-d'Olt
Rodez

BOURBONNAIS
0 20 40 60 km
ALLIER
CREUSE
LOIRE
FOREZ
LIMOUSIN
PUY-DE-DÔME
CORRÈZE
HAUTE-LOIRE
VELAY
CANTAL
BASSE-AUVERGNE
HAUTE-AUVERGNE
LOT
AVEYRON
AUBRAC
ROUERGUE
Sioule
Dordogne
Allier
Dore
Vézère
Corrèze
Maronne
Cère
Alagnon
Truyère
Bellaigue
Menat
St-Quintin
La Chapelle d'Andelot
St-Genès-du-Retz
Châteauneuf-les-B.
St-Hilaire-la-C.
Artonne
Montpensier
Vergheas
St-Georges-de-M.
St-Myon
Thuret
Jussat
Ris
Chateldon
Biollet
Comps
Combronde
St-André-le-C.
Luzillat
Maringues
Port-Ste-Marie
Mozac
Ennezat
Bulhon
Miremont
Volvic
Riom
Culhat
Montfermy
Marsat
Lezoux
Thiers
Pontaumur
St-Ours
Beauregard-l'E.
Néronde
Pontgibaud
Montferrand
Glaine-Montaigut
ymoutiers
Herment
Heume-l'Eglise
Chamalières
Pont-du-Ch.
Moissat-Bas
Aubusson-d'Auv.
Royat
Clermont-Fd
Chauriat
Courpière
Giroux
Orcival
Beaumont
Cournon
Le Crest
Billom
Neuville
Bourg-Lastic
St-Saturnin
Isserteau
St-Dier
reignac
Saulzet-le-F.
Cunlhat
St-Nectaire
Yronde
Manglieu
Messeix
La Bourboule
Champeix
Issoire
Sauxillanges
Ambert
Tauves
Le Mont-Dore
St-Diéry
Ronzières
Usson
Ussel
Chastreix
Le Chambon-s-L.
Jonas
Colamine-ss-V.
Mailhat
St-Germain-L'H.
Meymac
Bagnols
Besse-en-Ch.
Orsonnette
Marsac-en-L.
Vassivière
Nonette
St-Bonnet-le-B.
Arlanc
Bort-les-Orgues
St-Donat
Chalus
Lanobre
Picherande
Vignonet
Roche-Charles
Champagnac
Compains
Dore-l'Eglise
Vebret
Egliseneuve-d'E.
Ydes
Saignes
La Godivelle
Sauvat
Menet
Vendes
Trizac
Vèze
Riom-ès-M.
Allanche
Massiac
Moussages
Jaleyrac
St-Hippolyte
Vernols
Vauclair
Chalvignac
Le Vigean
La Font-Sainte
Cheylade
Ste-Anastasie
ubazine
Mauriac
Tourniac
Dienne
Chalinargues
Anglards-de-S.
Brageac
Cussac-X.
Chastel-s-M.
Pleaux
St-Bonnet-de-S.
St-Paul
Ally
Salers
Bredons
St-Christophe
Coltines
Andelat
St-Martin-C.
Tournemire
Valuéjols
Roffiac
St-Flour
St-Cernin
St-Cirgues-de-J.
Girgols
Beaulieu-sur-Dordogne
Lascelle
Brezons
Alleuze
Montvert
Laroquevieille
Vic-s-Cère
Aurillac
Jou-ss-M.
St-Etienne-de-C.
Chaudes-Aigues
ocamadour
Rouziers
Montsalvy
Maurs
St-Urcize
hors
oissac
Conques
Auvergne
CHER
NIÈVRE
INDRE
SAÔNE ET LOIRE
ALLIER
CREUSE
PUY de DÔME
LOIRE
CORRÈZE
CANTAL
HAUTE-LOIRE
LOT
LOZÈRE
ARDÈCHE
AVEYRON
Romanesque or partially Romanesque church, treasure or place of pilgrimage
Orcival Site mentioned in the text or illustrated
Alleuze Another Romanesque site

GLOSSARY

Abacus: stone moulding or carving that forms the top of a capital on which the arch springer is laid to support the pillar or column.
Absidiole: a small apse forming the rear of chapels.
Aisle: a side nave of a church when the height of its vaulting is less than that of the main central nave.
Ambulatory: a gallery running around the choir of a church and which connects the side aisles.
Andesite: grey or black igneous rock of the diorite family.
Apse: a semi-circular domed termination to the choir in churches without ambulatories.
Arcading: a series of small, decorated, intersecting arcades.
Arch moulding: a small arch covering the recess of a splayed portal, that is recessed in the wall.
Arkose: a sedimentary rock that resembles a hard, yellowish sandstone.
Atlante: a male figure on a capital that appears to be supporting the springer.
Axial chapel: a chapel opening on to the axis of the choir and the nave.
Barlong (block): the rectangular support of the bell tower over the transept crossing, the longest side of which is perpendicular to that of the church.
Barrel: the semi-circular vault so characteristic of Romanesque architecture.
Bay: any opening, door or window, whether closed by a door or glass.
Bay: longitudinal part of the nave or aisle between two support.
Bell gable: a gable wall the top of which has bays in which bells are hung.
Billets (rows of): a series of ornamental motifs made up of semi-cylindrical stones the spacing distance of which equals their length.
Buttress: additional pillars arranged outside the church to absorb the thrust of the arches.
Capital: the top of a column, pillar or pilaster where the support joins the load.
Cella: that part of primitive shrines that contained the effigy of Christ.
Chapter house: the room in which the chapter of canons or other clerics gathered.
Chevet: that part of the church outside at the end of the nave, behind the choir and which corresponds to the apse.
Choir: originally intended to accommodate liturgical singers, the extension of the central nave beyond the transept crossing, containing the altar.
Column: a circular support.
Crossing (transept): a square or rectangular space determined by the intersection of the nave and the transept.
Crypt: a normally subterranean chamber under the East end of the church, intended to keep relics.
Cupola: hemispherical vault.
Diaphragm arch: an arch supporting a wall between two internal parts of the church, particularly between the nave and the crossing.
East facing (absidioles or chapels): said of chapels the longitudinal axis of which runs East – West and the end of which faces East.
Engaged column: a semi-circular column built on a pillar or wall.
Evangelary: a book containing the four Gospels read or sung during Mass all year long.
Ex-voto: a tablet bearing an evocative inscription or object left on a pilgrimage site after taking a vow or in thanks for a prayer answered.
Gable: a wall, the top of which support the peak of the roof and forms an isosceles triangle.
Glory (in): a representation of Christ of the Virgin Mary, face on, generally seated on a throne in a stylised formal pose.
Half barrel: a vault forming a quarter cylinder, so typical of the Romanesque galleries and side aisles in Basse Auvergne.
Head reliquary: the head or bust of a Saint and which contains his or her relics.
Hinge: flat iron band fixed to the leaf of a door to secure it to the pintle.
In the round: sculpture which is detached from the bottom, the opposite of bas-relief.
Mandorla: an oval shape containing Christ in glory at the Last Judgement.
Modillions: small stone brackets supporting the cornice of a roof.
Narthex: another name for vestibule, a room at the West end of the nave and side aisles and separate from them. Originally set aside for catechumens not yet baptised who could not go further into the church.
Pendentive: a squinch formed by the triangular segment of a spherical surface.
Phonolite: compact igneous rock (feldspar trachyte) which makes a ringing sound when struck.
Pier: door upright supporting the lintel.
Pilaster: flat engaged pillar in a wall.
Pillar: a square or rectangular support which is larger than a column.
Pointed barrel: a barrel vault, the apex of which forms a re-entrant angle.
Porch: the entrance to a church which open out through bays without doors.
Radiating chapels: chapels the longitudinal axis of which is the radius of a circle formed by the ambulatory into which they open and the centre of which is the choir.
Reliquary: a chest in which the relics of a Saint are kept.
Rock hewn: hewn from or painted on bare rock.
Roofing stones: flat stones of phonolite, schist or gneiss, used for roofing in mountainous regions.
Round end: a semi-circular series of columns which separate the ambulatory from the choir.
Round: used for semi-circular arches so characteristic of Romanesque architecture.
Saddle (lintel): a two-sided roof shape.
Semi cupola: a quarter sphere vault over the apses and absidioles.
Side aisles: side naves of a church.
Squinch: small arch support in the corners of the square of the crossing to form a circular support for the cupola that covers it.
Statue reliquary: a statue with a cavity intended to contain relics.
Trachyte: a hard, rough igneous rock generally grey-red in colour.
Transept (arm) or crossing: the areas at the North and South ends of the transept.
Transept: a transverse nave which cuts the central nave of a church and which gives it its symbolic cross shape.
Transverse arch: an arch built under the barrel vault.
Trefoiled: in the shape of a clover leaf.
Tribunes: in Romanesque architecture, galleries looking on to the central nave between the arcades of the aisles and the upper windows.
Trilobate: having three lobes.
Triumphal arch: the arch separating the central nave from the transept or choir.
Tuff: light, porous volcanic rock.
Tympanum: that part of a wall occupying the semi-circle between the lintel and the arch above the main doors of a church.
Voussoirs: wedge shaped stones used in the construction of lintels, vaults and cornices.

INDEX

Odinary type, pages with text - ***Bold type, pages with illustrations.***

Backpage, *Christ in glory at Brioude (Haute-Loire).*
Unboundcover, *the church of Saint Nectaire (Puy-de-Dôme) ;*
boundcover, *the chevet of Saint Austremoine at Issoire (Puy-de-Dôme);*
back unboundcover, *the Madonna of Vauclair (Cantal),* text by François Graveline ;
back boundcover, *the cloister of Lavaudieu (Haute-Loire).*

Déjà parus aux
Éditions Debaisieux

Le puy de Dôme
& la chaîne des volcans
ISBN 2-913381-06-5 - 2e édition

Volcans des monts Dore
ISBN 2-9509180-8-5 - 2e édition

Cantal la saga d'un volcan
ISBN 2-913381-21-9

La Corrèze
2e édition augmentée de 16 pages
ISBN 2-9509180-9-3 broché
ISBN 2-913381-00-6 relié

Volcans célèbres & méconnus
du Massif central
ISBN 2-913381-03-0 broché français
ISBN 2-913381-04-9 relié français
ISBN 2-913381-12-X broché allemand
ISBN 2-913381-13-8 broché anglais

Le Puy-en-Velay
Ferveur, couleurs & bonheurs
ISBN 2-913381-18-9 broché français
ISBN 2-913381-19-7 broché allemand
ISBN 2-913381-20-0 broché anglais

Auvergne, Bourbonnais & Velay
ISBN 2-913381-14-6 broché français
ISBN 2-913381-15-4 relié français
ISBN 2-913381-16-2 broché allemand
ISBN 2-913381-17-0 broché anglais

Les plus beaux volcans
Auvergne, Aubrac & Velay
ISBN 2-9509180-7-7

Les plus beaux châteaux
Auvergne, Bourbonnais & Velay
ISBN 2-913381-01-4

Vierges romanes
ISBN 2-913381-02-2

Fleurs familières & méconnues
du Massif central
ISBN 2-913381-05-7

Contes & saveurs d'Auvergne
ISBN 2-913381-07-3

We should like to thank warmly all those who have given their time in preparing this work together with Bibliothèque Municipale InterUniversitaire de Clermont-ferrand and Editions Zodiaque.

2e édition enrichie de 16 pages, achevée d'imprimer en France en mai 2002 - Dépot légal mai 2002
ISBN 2-913381-08-1 version brochée française - ISBN 2-913381-09-X version reliée française
(1ère édition ISBN 2-9509180-5-0 version brochée - ISBN 2-9509180-6-9 version reliée)
Versions étrangères achevées d'imprimer en France en mai 2002 - Dépot légal mai 2002
ISBN 2-913381-10-3 version brochée allemande - ISBN 2-913381-11-1 version brochée anglaise

rue Becquerel - Z.A. de l'Artière - F 63110 Beaumont
Téléphone 33 (0)4 73 27 43 00 - Fax 33 (0) 4 73 26 26 12
www.editions-debaisieux.fr